About the Author

Liz Dean is the author of 18 books and card decks, including *Nature's Hidden Oracles*, *The Ultimate Guide to Tarot*, *Game of Thrones Tarot*, *The Magic of Tarot* and *Switchwords: How to Use One Word to Get What You Want*. She has taught at the Omega Institute, New York; in Perth, Melbourne and Sydney for the Tarot Guild of Australia; and at the London Tarot Conference and London Tarot Festival. Her current areas of interest include intuitive symbol reading, divination in nature, poetry, and tarot as creative practice. She lives by the sea in Roker, Sunderland, in north-east England.

www.lizdean.info
Twitter.com/lizdeanbooks
Instagram.com/lizdeanbooks

Nature's Hidden Charms

50 Signs, Symbols & Practices from the Natural World
to Bring Inner Peace, Protection & Good Fortune

Liz Dean

Illustrations by Lizzie Harper

WELBECK
BALANCE

A Trigger Book
Published by Welbeck Balance
An imprint of Welbeck Publishing Group
20 Mortimer Street
London W1T 3JW

First published by Welbeck Balance in 2021

A CIP catalogue record for this book is available from the British Library

ISBN
Trade Hardback – 978-1-78956-305-4

Designed by Kathryn Davies
Typeset by Lapiz Digital Services
Printed and Bound in China

10 9 8 7 6 5 4 3 2 1

Note/Disclaimer

www.welbeckpublishing.com

For all those who wander in nature

Foreword

This timely book offers a ready introduction to our dependence on nature for our physical and mental wellbeing. It offers insights into the cultural history of folk practices and beliefs, many of which can still be found today. It also serves as an aid to anyone who wants to get more out of their daily walk, explaining how to tune in to the finer details of the natural world, whether in the local park or a distant forest.

Who among us hasn't picked up a feather from the hedgerow, or made a wish on the pull of a chicken bone, or carried a smooth flat pebble in our pocket while we try and figure out some tricky problem? And who hasn't tossed a coin into a public fountain? But what are we doing when we make these small but focused interactions with the natural world? Until relatively recently, there were thousands of sacred wells and springs across Europe where we made our wishes and gave thanks, and many still remain, such as the Chalice Well at Glastonbury, or the Tobernalt Well in Sligo.

While many of these old places have disappeared, the same practices have simply reappeared in urban settings. The proof is in the sparkle of coins that wink back at us from civic fountains everywhere. The annual haul from the Trevi Fountain in Rome is estimated to be around US$1.5million, an indication that these traditions remain as popular as ever.

No matter that most of us live in cities, nature continues to play an important part in our lives, contributing to our sense of wellbeing, now and for the future. Next to most medieval churches grows the evergreen yew. This pairing is so familiar that we may never stop to question why. Venture into the church and you will most likely find a stone font. Within its bowl can be found a smooth wooden disc – this is merely the end of a long rod that reaches right into the ground. Early churches were often built next to sacred wells or in sacred glades, and when Christianity was introduced, the symbols of our reverence for nature were brought inside the building. When we baptise our children in the blessed waters of the stone font, with its rooting into the earth, we sum up our relationship with the natural world: we are of it, and it is of us, both spiritually and physically, and we will depend on it from infancy until old age. This conjunction of faith and water is not uniquely Christian, and ritual immersion in still or flowing waters can be found in many faiths – no more so than Hinduism, where the sacred Ganges river is considered to be the *tirtha* or bridge between this world and the next.

As the most noble forms of vegetation, trees also feature large in spiritual practices. In ancient Greece, men and women sought to learn their future from the wind rustling through the oak trees at the Oracle of Dodona. In Japan, Shinto shrines are set among groves of sacred cryptomeria trees. Across Europe, the Maypole, once the centre of spring festivities, which included dances such as "strip the willow", have much in common with the traditions of the Blackfoot tribes of North America, in which a sapling is stripped of all but its uppermost foliage and set up as the focal point of a great seasonal gathering.

"Trees, water, stone: they are ubiquitous in nature and in timeless rites and practices to be found across the world."

Close by the Bronze Age circle of standing stones at Avebury, Wiltshire, you will find an ancient oak hanging with coloured rags or "clooties", each tied to express a desire of something to come, or in gratitude for a wish granted. Go to Lindisfarne, or take the road to Santiago de Compostela, or hike any long-distance trail and you will see cairns of carefully piled stones. These are indications of the inner, as well as the physical journeys, of those who have passed along the way.

Within the pages of this book can be found scores of examples of how we have traditionally connected with nature. Finding space for contemplation doesn't always need a major expedition up a mountain or to a distant shrine. A walk through a local park, or heathland, or beach, offers an opportunity to contemplate whatever is of concern that day.

In this book, Liz Dean offers guidance on how to focus our thoughts through the detailed consideration of small, natural objects we might find on such walks, and how to make the most of the natural world around us. After all, though we exist in nature, it exists in us too. In one of his many journals, the great naturalist and wilderness prophet, John Muir, wrote, "I only went out for a walk and finally concluded to stay out till sundown, for going out, I found, was really going in."[i]

Victoria Preston
Author of *We are Pilgrims*

---

i   Muir, J, ed. L M Wolfe (1938), *John of the Mountains: The Unpublished Journals of John Muir.*

Contents

Introduction

From acorns in woodland to pebbles on the beach, we're drawn to hold a piece of nature. Our desire to seek treasures in nature runs deep in our psyche, as when we were hunter-gatherers scouring the land for food, firewood, bones for tools and amulets for protection. The fairy tales we heard as children are full of magical, transformation charms, from the bone used by Hansel and Gretel to trick their captor, to Snow White's poison apple. Today, as natural gatherers, we take home totems of our experience to keep alive the memories of our walks, all the while holding a feeling that there is somehow more to it. A feather, a stone, a flower, a leaf – these are natural charms that carry significance beyond the literal. We collect them to remind ourselves of a special experience, a person or a place; where we were; who, if anyone, we were with; the turn of the season; the way it rained on the way home; how the rainbow's haze appeared from the drizzle. Charms are often receptacles for our memories and our hopes.

Walking in nature is a call to reconnect with nature's cycles, and to enjoy a deeper relationship with the natural world – to be a part of it, rather than an onlooker admiring flowers from behind the park railings. And through charms, those tiny pieces of the whole, we can make a start. Charms open us up to sensory experience and, through this, a real sense of connection with nature and reconnection with the self – bringing serenity, self-empowerment, healing and wish-fulfilment.

"A charm is hope, a living symbol of your wishes."

Nature is sensational medicine. When you stop to really look at a herb sprig, a fallen twiglet or a shell, you sense its elemental energy. You see its detail, and notice a vague scent – lavender, earth, salt. The shape, colour and pattern become immersive, and spark your imagination; it's impossible to flit back to the mindset you had before your walk because your senses are suddenly open and conversing with the land, the trees, the charm in your hand. You become present in the moment. Stress fades away and curiosity steps in – you're drawn to the intricate fluting on a leaf-edge or the tiny holes in a white stone. Perception shifts. One of our greatest modern challenges is stress and anxiety. When you go into nature, nature helps you reconnect with the part of you that knows how to heal.

A charm is hope, a living symbol of your wishes. The charms and the rituals of charm-making you choose are unique to you – they're a way to celebrate nature, and they enhance your awareness of what you need, going forward. You can dedicate a charm to assist in decision-making, letting go, problem-solving, positivity, meditation, love, creative projects and much, much more.

Charms operate through sympathetic magic – the way in which one object stands in for another. When we carry a charm or place it on display at home, it keeps its source properties. There's a sympathetic connection between two objects: the twig disassociated from the tree still holds the power of the tree. The feather found on the sand possesses the innate qualities of the bird it once belonged to. This relationship between the piece and its origin, the small and the large, gives many charms their meanings. Many traditional charm meanings are included in this book, but you're encouraged to intuit your own, and work with them in rituals to create positive changes in your life.

Through the many ideas, techniques and practices in the following pages, this book invites you to take a sensory journey into a garden, a park, the woods, a lakeside, or any wild places, to powerfully reconnect with nature, and with your wild, creative self.

So, take a breath, venture out – and prepare to be charmed.

HOW TO USE THIS BOOK

This book includes a host of practices – activities to try out in nature and at home. Loosely termed "techniques" and "rituals", their purpose is to help you connect with nature at a spiritual level. Techniques show you how to approach a task or learn a skill, such as collecting finds or communing with a plant, whereas rituals focus on particular charm projects.

You can read through the chapters before or during your walk, or intuitively choose a technique or ritual: take a breath, close your eyes and ask to see the practice you most need at this time. Flick through the pages and stop when it feels right to do so. The practice nearest your stopping page is the one for you today.

In the first chapter, we look at how those who came before us used natural charms, and the endurance of popular ones such as the four-leaved clover and the corn dolly, along with concepts of protection and enchantment.

In Chapter 2, you can explore the techniques and approaches for walking in the wild – what to look for, what to bring, how to connect with your finds and how to dedicate and make combination charms.

In Part 2, Chapters 3 to 9 are your core resource, as they are arranged by charm type: trees; fruits, nuts and seeds; herbs; grasses and vines; stones; shells and seaweed; and eggshells and feathers.

To discover how to work with sacred shapes, turn to Chapter 10, which gives you ways to make a charm circle, spiral, tree, infinity symbol, *vesica piscis* (two intersecting circles) and pentagram for a home altar or outside, if you have a garden or a yard.

Chapter 11 shows how to interpret your charms in terms of their number symbolism and see the significance of numbers in counting charms.

IMPORTANT NOTES

TERMINOLOGY

In this book, the words "charm" and "find" are used interchangeably to refer to any natural object you find and feel drawn to. "Charm" encompasses amulets and talismans (protective charms are amulets; wish-granting charms, often made at special times, are generally thought of as talismans). A charm can also be a poem or a rhyme, spoken as part of a "ritual". A ritual is a sequence of actions undertaken to express devotion, make a spiritual connection or request, and, broadly, to honour life in all its forms.

ACCESS TO NATURE

Always be respectful of nature. Take only small items, or small amounts of leaves, shells, feathers or other finds. Follow the local rules – for example, some authorities may not allow you to take home pebbles

5

and shells from their beaches because their removal may cause environmental damage. It may, however, be permissible to carry something for the duration of your walk and leave it behind before you go. If in doubt, check with the relevant authorities or landowners before you take anything.

If you're not allowed to pick up or take anything from an area, you can use the rituals in this book that don't depend on collecting an object. You can take a photograph (again, if permitted), draw, write and connect through sight.

Note that you don't need access to woodlands, countryside or beaches in order to carry out the activities in this book, because you can adapt them for your own local environment. Or, if you prefer, you can read about them here and then do them when you next visit a forest, the countryside, the beach or other suitable setting.

SAFETY

Avoid handling plants, fungi, berries and anything else that may be toxic or otherwise unsafe to smell, touch or eat. If in doubt, do NOT touch and certainly do NOT eat them! You can still connect with them from a distance (see page 42).

SUSTAINABILITY

When you are out looking for and collecting charms, be very mindful of the environment. Often the advice given is to "leave no more than a footprint" after your visit, and you should always leave the woods, the countryside or the beach as you find it.

Do not pick growing leaves, buds and flowers – you can usually find some that have fallen naturally from the tree or plant. Avoid stacking stones and, before taking any objects, consider the impact of your actions on the sustainability of the landscape or their role in providing food and shelter for wildlife. Don't take anything non-biodegradable with you and never leave behind anything to pollute nature.

There's an old saying that for whatever you take from nature – even just a leaf or two – you should give the fairies something back. A few strands of your hair will do, because, as the saying goes, the fairies will make use of it. On the same note, if you take something, make an exchange, such as by collecting any litter you see.

PART ONE

Finding Your Way

In this part, we look not just at the charms that lead us back into folk tradition – the four-leaved clover, hare's foot and corn dolly – but those lesser-known charms that have other stories to tell about the beliefs of their bearers.

We will also discover the techniques needed to seek out charms – beginning with ways to heighten sensory awareness to commune with a tree, a plant, an object or a place – and to make unique charms in nature or at home, from pine cones to shells, and from pebbles to grasses and feathers. There's also an intuitive guided activity showing how one charm can guide us from place to place, opening up new experiences in favourite places.

1

Charms of Old

Our ancestors made charms for protection, courage, luck and magic from the natural materials around them – wood, bone, animal skin, shell, stone, herbs and feathers. When we walk through the forest, roam on the moor or follow the hedgerows, we become part of an ancient desire to positively influence the present and the future. Charms were a key ingredient in survival and protection, and our needs today are perhaps not so different.

ANIMAL CHARMS

Animal totems were highly prized in early cultures. Owning a piece of an animal was to possess part of its spirit; a feline claw, like that of a panther, was a charm for courage; a shark's tooth protected the wearer from accident or poison; and a fox tongue was thought to make the bearer bold and brave, just like the intrepid fox itself. While much of what we know about animal charms has been passed down to us through folklore, many animal charms survive in physical form – tangible proof of their vital role in survival. The fox tongue and shark's tooth are part of the collection of William James Clarke (1871–1945), an English folklorist whose cache of rarities includes a charm against conception (the inner ear of a codfish) and tiny mole's feet, used to combat toothache. Like mini time-capsules, these preserved charms reveal our ancestors' hopes and fears.

"When we walk through the forest, roam on the moor or follow the hedgerows, we become part of an ancient desire to positively influence the present and the future."

A Viking locket found in Gotland, Sweden, contains the remains of a small but whole coiled snake. We might assume that the keeper of the locket killed the snake or was given it by someone who did. The snake-locket was likely a portable charm against poisoning or other misfortune, while the snake as a symbol hints at a deeper, magical purpose. The dragon, its mythical ancestor, takes a key role in Norse mythology as the Midgard Serpent, which encircled the earth in a binding spell, and as Fafnir, the once-human dragon vanquished by his brother, Sigurd. When Sigurd drinks Fafnir's blood, he gains supernatural powers.

Bones are both literal evidence and a metaphor for truth. Swearing on the bones of the ancestors is to declare an absolute, so dedicating a bone as a charm declared true purpose as it was sure to work. Bones were carried to bring strength, and also good fortune – for example, a bone from a sheep skull was seen as lucky, with the bonus of protecting the owner from witchcraft. The chicken wishbone for luck is an echo of this bone tradition. Two people pull on each fork of the bone to break it, all the while making a silent wish. The person who gets the most bone when it snaps gets the luck.

Pagan Anglo-Saxon graves often contained animal bones and shells, and women's graves in particular housed amulets (protective charms) that included boar tusks, horse teeth and cowrie shells (the shiny, coiled shells that were historically used as currency). Paganism scholar Ronald Hutton suggests that the cowrie shell symbolized female genitalia, while the boar tusks were a lunar symbol, also denoting femininity.[1]

Bones were used in prophesying, too: in Hoodoo or root work, the magical practice originating in Africa, bone divination is still practised today. This type of divination has other cultural roots – a shoulder blade of an ox dating to 1300–1050 BCE from China's Henan province features a pattern of cracks in the bone caused by heating, which the diviner would interpret. In England, the Museum of Witchcraft in Cornwall has the shoulder blade of a rabbit pierced with nine pins for use in divination.

"Bones are both literal evidence and a metaphor for truth. Swearing on the bones of the ancestors is to declare an absolute, so dedicating a bone as a charm declared true purpose as it was sure to work."

THE HARE AND THE RABBIT

The hare's foot and tail, or those of the rabbit, were popular charms during the first half of the 20th century. Some were carried generally for luck, and others were used in English folk magic. An exhibit from 1936 in the Museum of Witchcraft in Cornwall consists of a hare's foot wrapped in paper that has magical symbols drawn on it. The description reads, "Hare's foot. Bound with a parchment charm made by a sorcerer in order to cure a farmer who had injured his leg while foxhunting."[2] Another charm, housed at the Scarborough Museum in Yorkshire, is a hare's tail used by a fisherman to bring in a good catch.

There's always been a magical air about the hare, perhaps due to the way the animal "flies" – its hind legs land before its front legs, so all four paws are momentarily off the ground.

Or maybe because, like the rabbit, the hare is born with its eyes open, which in early times signified it was protected from the "evil eye". Its most potent association, however, is its place in nature as the harbinger of spring. Our ancestors recognized the hare as a fertility symbol of the goddess Éostre, or Easter, and its ability to reproduce quickly led to the Roman idea of hares as symbols of lust and fertility. As ever, charms came in and out of fashion – before hare's feet and tails became commercially available at the turn of the last century, the hare had a darker meaning as a portent of disaster. In the 19th century, the following protection charm involved spitting over the left shoulder before reciting:

"Hare before,
Trouble behind:
Change ye,
Cross, and free me."

ELVES, FAIRIES, WITCHES AND
THE EVIL EYE

Every kind of evil necessitated every kind of charm. From potions against naughty fairies to healing salves and spoken charms or incantations, our ancestors employed whatever they had to hand – along with practices passed down the generations – to ward off negative influences. The Anglo-Saxon nine-herb charm (see page 221) lists nine herbs that "have power against nine evil spirits/Against nine poisons and nine infections."

> "There is a suggestion that knots were used to deter fairies, as if cure and cause were one and the same."

From medieval texts to folk magic and common superstition, the concept of "evil" is personified according to culture and belief. In the Anglo-Saxon period, elves were considered largely to blame for illnesses, along with "flying venom" (airborne diseases). By the Middle Ages, fairies loomed large in human consciousness, often as dangerous agents of disruption who could steal children and replace them with changelings. By the 17th century and the witch trials, the witch was the most prominent personification of evil (although, ironically, these women were the victims of exactly what they were accused of doing). These so-called faces of evil have co-existed over the centuries and played centre-stage according to the spirit of the age and the influence of the Church. Moreover, you couldn't always blame the supernaturals:

it was believed that humans, too, could give the evil eye – a catch-all term for all sorts of misfortune.

According to scholar Wendy Rouse[3], "The concept of the evil eye appears to have originated in the Mediterranean region thousands of years ago and became widespread throughout the Middle East, Europe and later the Americas, with the expansion of Western civilisations." A person with the evil eye could intentionally or accidentally harm your child or destroy your livestock with just one look. Random misfortune needed an explanation, a source, whether elf, fairy, witch, demon or human.

In English folklore, elves and fairies were renowned for their tricks. One farmer in Cornwall, England, woke to find his horse's mane knotted with "fairy stirrups" because fairies had been riding the horse at night. He had "no doubt that at least twenty small people had sat upon the horse's neck," and that "the piskie (Cornish pixie) people had been riding Tom again"[4]. In one account reported by Walter Scott, a man "found his hair was tied in double knots (well known by the name of elf-locks) and that he had almost lost his speech." There is also a suggestion that knots were used to deter fairies, as if cure and cause were one and the same. Folklore collector Thomas Westropp relates how "Seven hairs were knotted in the mane of a horse or the tail of a cow to protect against fairies."[5] In this instance, the knots acted as a kind of magical antibiotic. We see the same with witches: the hawthorn bush guarded against witches, although witches were believed to shape-shift into hawthorn bushes. As Desmond Morris in his charm compendium *Bodyguards* explains, the witch-tree could be depended on to catch a fellow witch.

"The rowan tree's folkloric associations include divination and psychic protection."

A rowan tree inscribed with a cross, or "witch post", was known to keep witches away, yet the rowan's folkloric associations include divination and psychic protection. Gnarls and knots on trees were reportedly the heads of dead witches, trapped forever in the trunks.

As English wise women became tainted and persecuted, perceived threat lay everywhere: even a wander through woodland could put a soul in danger – and so the witch became the wolf, lying in wait for Red Riding Hood.

THE POPULARITY OF RITUALS

If we consider that making medicine from nature was a kind of magic that brought about healing, it followed that similar rituals could be metaphysical cures for spiritual afflictions. Herbs, bark, stones, shells, cones and fruits were gathered, just like herbal cures, and were used in a ritual – including a sung charm – to ward off danger and bring luck. It seemed that luck and protection were one and the same: if you were protected, you were also lucky.

There were hundreds of ways to gain good luck, from seeing rainbows to finding white feathers, which suggests that luck might be accumulated as protection against plague, accidents, a bad harvest, stillbirths, lightning, fire, animal attack, infant death, robbery and spinsterhood – all those ever-present threats to survival. Plants, stones and shells became even luckier if they had something distinctive about them. If you were lucky enough to find a four-leaved clover, you'd soon attract your future wife or husband. The power of the quatrefoil (four leaves) also leapt from the plant to its owner – Elizabethan folklore had it that just holding a four-leaved clover meant you would see fairies and, even better, could ask the fairies to grant you a wish. Its three-leaved sister still brought happiness, though – the leaves stood for faith, hope and love, and the trefoil had its own history, venerated as it was by the Tuatha Dé Danann, Ireland's mythical tribe of gods.

"Rituals help combat fear and soothe the anxiety of the unknown."

An odd-looking whelk shell in the Science Museum in London[6] was once used as a charm because it is left-handed – its spiral is reversed, a relatively rare find. The charm came from a fish porter at Billingsgate fish market, London, who kept it as a totem to protect his health. Shells represent protection and love, but the reversed spiral shell was precious, and presumably because of its rarity, its power was greater, giving the owner what he most desired – enough vitality to keep working.

We may see this type of ritual as archaic, but ritual is part of us. Wearing a favourite piece of jewellery, a "lucky" tie, even setting a table for dinner – each habit is a hope for a favourable outcome. In this way, rituals helped combat fear and soothe the anxiety of the unknown. Rituals are intended to generate a feeling of safety by symbolically exerting control over what is ultimately out of our control, whether it's illness, other people or the weather. In this sense, the ritual itself was as important as the goal.

CORN DOLLIES AND ONION DOLLS

In English agricultural communities, the corn dolly was a traditional feature of many a household after harvest. If you took a small sheaf of corn, bound it under the corn-ears and added plaited corn for arms, you had a fertility charm or idol (doll is short for idol). This practice stems from a belief in the corn-spirit, which would fly into the last of the growing corn when the field was being harvested. This last corn was made into a doll, preserving the indwelling corn spirit. The dollies were kept until spring, when their grain was planted to begin the cycle of fertility again. The corn spirit was personified and called the corn mother, the harvest queen, the hag or Old Woman, and displayed in the house to celebrate harvest-time and bring luck for the next harvest. The last corn was also made into other shapes, such as hearts, fans and twists, known as harvest tokens.

"Objects and their stories lead us to see the world through other eyes for a moment, and sometimes these perspectives can be wildly different."

Chris Gosden, in his *History of Magic*, relates a tale of the humble onion being ritually employed by a publican called Samuel Porter to ward off a family called Fox, who were members of the Temperance movement. He wrote the name of a family member on a piece of paper and wrapped each paper around an onion, securing it with pins. The publican made the onion dolls to stop the Fox family putting him out of business. The totems were hung inside the Barley Mow pub's chimney in Somerset, England, and left to dry out – symbolically drying up the bodies of his adversaries. As Gosden says, "The onion was a small and unlikely weapon in the battle between those convinced of the evils of drink and those wishing to sell and consume liquor."[7] One onion is preserved, dated 1872, in the Pitt Rivers Museum, Oxford, England.

MULTIPLE MEANINGS

From folklore, charms in museum collections, and songs and practices passed down through the generations, we get multiple glimpses of the past. Objects and their stories lead us to see the world through other eyes for a moment, and sometimes these perspectives can be wildly different. In plant lore, this variance is often reflected in the number of colloquial names for a plant. Yarrow, for example, has more than 20 names: from sneezewort to soldier's woundwort, devil's nettle to seven years' love, which reveal many of the herb's legendary properties. The mythic story of yarrow tells how the god Achilles used it to heal soldiers' wounds in the Trojan war (its Latin name is *Achillea millefolium*). In domestic life, placing yarrow in a milk churn kept the milk from going sour. In Scotland, yarrow leaves placed over the eyes made you psychic. In Ireland, yarrow sewn into clothing brought a person luck. In China, the divination system *I Ching* uses yarrow stalks. But then, the Welsh knew yarrow as the death flower; if brought into the house, funerals surely followed.

At one level, these tales of yarrow are testament to the versatility of plants for healing and luck. At another level, they suggest that knowledge was localized. People worked with the natural charms in their environment, and meanings developed based on their personal experiences. Perhaps, in a part of Wales, yarrow became linked with death by association because it happened to be present in a household just before a family member died. Again, we were, and are, always looking to explain the inexplicable. By making something taboo, we create ritual and through that ritual, hoped-for protection.

2

Charm-seeking

When you are open to communicating with the natural world, you intuitively choose the charms that work for you. If you take a sensory approach to your walk, pathways of communication open up – you know when a charm is right for you and sense what it can do.

"You may think you walk in silence, but when you go into nature you're joining a live conversation, tapping into a unique and ancient resonance."

In folklore, the idea of plant, animal and mineral communication is deeply embedded. Birds talk to trees, and trees talk to one another and to humans. In the Buckinghamshire tale *The Juniper Tree*, junipers are known gossips, "nearly as bad as pine trees, and they get bored very quickly."[8] Folk stories fictionalize physical reality. Trees "converse" by sending chemical signals via networks of roots and thread-like fungi to warn of drought or disease.[9] When an insect nibbles at a leaf, the plant emits a chemical to tell other plants to increase their defence response. Cut grass emits an aroma that signals danger to other plants in the vicinity. Plants share their wisdom with one another; a chatter you can sense when you make your way from the known world of home to the ever-changing world of nature. There's an intangible feeling that you're entering another reality, an alternative level of consciousness. The air takes on a new scent and the hum of traffic gives way to the breath of the wind. You notice the shift in tone, and feel it in your bones. You may think you walk in silence, but when you go into nature you're joining a live conversation, tapping into a unique and ancient resonance.

OPENING THE SENSES

To connect with nature we work through our senses and emotions. To do this, we pay close attention to how certain areas of nature and its plants and trees make us feel. In this feeling mode, we open up to intuition, imagination and creativity. We experience oneness – a feeling of unity within and a sense of being part of nature's whole.

Stephen Buhner notes that "When sensory gating channels are widely opened, the boundary between self and other thins."[10] Experiencing nature through your senses dissolves the barrier that casts you as the observer, the visitor who must remain distant. In sensory mode, being in nature is immersive. Without inner conflict or feelings of separation, we find peace and space. I see Buhner's "thinning" as the dissolving of tension we experience when we feel anxious or overwhelmed with thoughts. We're not telling ourselves that it's good to be outdoors and that we should enjoy it; we're just as we are, in the natural world, in a state of being. In this being-state we're fully present and open to receiving the sensory impressions around us, and our senses open the gateway to a conversation with nature. We listen, respond, and make meaning from what we see, hear and feel. This is the charm-seeking sensibility – to see the walk as a journey from one state to another, and an opportunity to connect with nature and with ourselves. Then, we're guided toward the charms we need.

TECHNIQUE
Going for Your First Guided Walk

This activity will guide you through finding your first charms, which is the basis of all charm-work. You will then be able to move on to learn how to dedicate them and connect with their energy later in the chapter.

Where to Go

You might have access to what we imagine as "true" or wild nature: rugged moors or acres of woodland, miles of cornfields or a stunning bay. Beautiful, if so – but nature is everywhere, and in places that sound less romantic, but which are more accessible day to day. Wherever you live, nature is not far away, even in urban settings. You can find it in city parks, garden centres and cemeteries. You'll have places you dream of and places on the doorstep, too. One tree in your yard or garden, for example, may give you all the charms you need – bark, twig, leaf, nut or cone.

What to Bring on Your Walk

- Pack a notebook, a pen and a selection of bags for your finds.
- Use a lightweight tote bag with a few smaller bags inside to store charms of different sizes. Choose cotton, linen or another natural fabric – natural charms need natural materials – rather than plastic (and damp leaves will also deteriorate in a small plastic bag).

- If you don't want to carry a bag, wear a coat with large, accessible pockets.
- If you bring along your phone, use it to take pictures of your finished mandalas or other temporary nature art. But until then, resist the temptation to take photographs. Work on building mental images and sensory impressions, and you'll have a more rewarding charm-walk.

Setting Your Intention

Begin with an attitude of openness and be willing to receive. Ask that you see what is right for you, and that you make a connection. Then, release this wish and turn your attention back to where you are now.

If your thoughts are getting in the way, visualize that you're placing your current thoughts on shelves to your left and right sides. There's a white space opening up in front of you; know that you can gently move into it.

Greeting the Land

If you're comfortable doing so, greet the land as you're about to begin your walk.

1. First, take one solid breath in and out, feeling the movement of your breath within you.
2. Move your attention to your feet and sense the ground below you.
3. Look around, take in the landscape and say a word or make a gesture.

These small acts of preparation acknowledge that what you're about to do is important.

Generating Gratitude

Gratitude opens up a connection to the earth and helps you move into sensory mode. Being grateful also helps if you're feeling anxious and you've found it hard to visualize putting your thoughts away – a headful of lists and concerns can block your connection with nature, so you feel distanced from what you see rather than a part of it. Just be grateful to be here now for however long you have. When you're saying thank you, you're thanking nature in advance and also thanking yourself for making the time for this walk (you probably didn't have time at all, but you created it). So, say thank you, take a breath and enter into the spirit of nature that awaits.

Heightening Your Senses

- As you walk, be mindful of your thoughts. Observe them come and go and switch your focus to what your senses are telling you. Your sensory impressions will soon dominate unwanted thoughts of the past or future, bringing you into the moment.
- Really look at what's before you. Watch how water flows and see the currents making different patterns, or how the crown of a tree makes a perfect curve. See how quickly change happens; nothing in nature is ever truly still.
- Close your eyes and tune in to the sounds around you. The longer you listen, the louder those sounds will become.
- If you find unwanted thoughts start creeping in, use one

of your senses to anchor you back to the moment. Touch a tree's bark, listen for birdsong, notice how the grass moves in the breeze.

- When you're present, you'll find you muse on what's happening now – you might ask yourself: *I wonder how that happens?* or *Does that bird sing all day or just at this time?* These are welcome thoughts of the present.

Thinking Big

Tune in to your breathing. Imagine every time you breathe in and out your energy field is expanding – there's a glow around you that gets bigger and bigger. This energy field is gentle, and it's like having extending antennae. The greater the reach of the antennae, the more sensory information you pick up. You become more aware of your skin, the air temperature and the particular energy signatures of the life growing around you.

Follow Your Feet ... Then Stop

You'll find that you're drawn to a particular place, plant, tree, stone or flower. Give yourself permission to follow your feet, walking and stopping whenever you choose. Look more closely. Here are some examples of what you might find:

Inland
- Leaves and grasses
- Twigs and small branches
- Herb sprigs
- Bark and wood chippings

- Cones, nutshells, nuts, sycamore seeds
- Flower heads and petals
- Seed heads, such as dandelion puff-balls
- Feathers
- Stones
- Bird bones
- Eggshells

On the Beach

- Seashells
- Crab shells or claws
- Seaweed
- Egg cases
- Pebbles
- Barnacles
- Sea glass (glass weathered by the sea)

Just take one or two items, if you have permission to do so. Where possible, choose leaves, herbs and flowers that have recently fallen; only pick them from the plant if they are wild and plentiful, and only take a small amount.

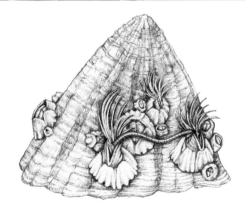

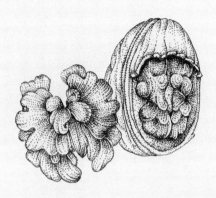

GETTING TO KNOW YOUR CHARM

You don't need to be able to formally identify what you see. When you're combing the beach, the woods or a park for natural treasures, it's about the impression your charm makes upon you. You may want to touch it (if safe to do so) or you may wish to simply gaze at it; you can gain much from observing and connecting – reading the energetic imprint (which we learn how to do later in this chapter – see pages 42–45), looking at its shape and colour, seeing how it's growing, and noticing the place where you found it. You may be drawn to pick up an object, a charm-to-be that has meaning for you. It might be a seed pod, a leaf, a shell, a twig, a feather, a nut, a stone or something else. As with people, you'll have an intuitive reaction.

Connect with your find exactly where you find it. If you've picked up a shell from the beach or a stone on a woodland path, don't pocket it, thinking you'll take a look at it later. Stay where you are and tune in on the spot. If you've found a fallen acorn under an oak, take the acorn to the tree and if possible, sit or stand with your back against it. Connecting with the parent tree helps you get a stronger link with your acorn. Tuning in straight away is a self-intervention – it keeps you spontaneous, going with the flow of your natural reactions. It's less likely that you'll over-think.

> "Tuning in to your charm straight away is a self-intervention – it keeps you spontaneous, going with the flow of your natural reactions. It's less likely that you'll over-think."

SINGLE OR COMBINATION?

You can use a single find as a charm or make a combined charm – this means two or more finds joined together and used as one. Do whatever feels right to you. For example, if you're attracted to one feather, that feather can become your charm. If you gather several items that you sense belong together – say, a stone, a nut and a leaf – you can tie them together to create a charm (see pages 46–47 for more on combining charms).

Now that you know the basics about going on an intuitive walk, we will look at a number of techniques for connecting with a find and reading its energy imprint.

UNDERSTANDING NATURAL ATTRACTION: OBSERVATION

Being in nature is a sensory experience, so let your sense of sight, rather than your thinking mind, lead you. The key is to pay attention to why you're fascinated by a particular find. See it as an investigation, and spend time making connections. The more connections you make, the stronger your relationship. The relationship you build with your find empowers it to become a charm unique to you.

Let's look at a couple of examples. Say you see some fallen red berries. It may not be wise to pick them up, because you don't know what they are, but you can safely gaze at them. You notice them because of their scarlet colour, their freshness. The colour has significance for you and it reminds you of David Hockney's work *The Arrival of Spring in Woldgate*, in which he paints a path through the forest in bright red. It speaks of new life and energy and also the enchantment of the forest and adventure that awaits. But you have your own personal connections to make. You liken the berries to blood droplets and the image gives you a metaphor – new blood. Perhaps that's what you're looking for at this time, what you'd like to embrace.

Or supposing you find that you're looking at a small stone – it's scratched and weathered. Small stones are often associated with travel, because they're easily scattered. The feeling you get from this find of yours is lightness; a need to explore an environment or situation unnoticed.

Now try it for yourself.

RITUAL
Communing with Your Charm through Observation

1. Choose or simply let yourself be drawn to a natural object. Ask yourself what it is about this particular item that attracts you.

2. Gaze at it very carefully and consider its characteristics. What form does it take? Is it round or elliptical? What is its texture? Is it rough or smooth? Does it have petals or hairs? If you've chosen a leaf or a flower head, the number of fronds or petals may hold meaning for you. For example, four protrusions suggest stability; three, creative energy (see Chapter 11 for more on the significance of numbers in nature).

3. As you scrutinize your charm, you may see a pattern on the surface that's beginning to appear the longer you gaze. What effect is this connection having on you? For example, is it soporific, edgy or energizing?

4. When you have communed with your charm for as long as you wish, speak aloud what you've discovered. This will make your mental impressions real and give them agency. Words give life to your experience.

We attract what we need, so whether your finds are strange, ugly, rare or beautiful, accept them, because they have unique meaning for you.

READING YOUR CHARM THROUGH TOUCH

Reading a natural object through touch is a form of psychometry – the art of reading the energy of objects through physical contact. Psychometry is usually practised with personal items, such as clothing or jewellery, which hold an energy-echo from the past. With natural finds, we're connecting with an object's living energy signature, a vibration that you can sense. It may feel strange doing this, and you may not get a feeling straight away.

> "We often receive guidance from nature when we don't have expectations or judgements. We can just be – and be open to what comes."

Give yourself time to let the impressions come. Don't worry that it's just your imagination; to imagine is to connect a feeling with an image. These images are symbols of our states of being and the "being" of the mineral, plant or animal find we're connecting to. We often receive guidance from nature when we don't have expectations or judgements. We can just be – and be open to what comes.

HEART RITUAL
Connecting through Touch

1. If it's safe to do so, hold your chosen find. Ask its permission, silently or aloud, and sense if you're welcome to continue. If it

doesn't feel right, gently return the object to where you found it and walk on. It if does feel right (your gaze or touch feels natural and comfortable, and/or and you feel an immediate "yes"), place your find in one palm and cup it with the other, so you have full contact. It's fine if your find doesn't fit into your palms – if you had a large feather, for example, it would extend beyond them. The aim is to have as much physical contact as you can.

2. Close your eyes and take a breath, taking your attention to your find. Does it feel warm, cool or cold? Rough, smooth or spiky? You may feel a gentle outward push, as if your stone, shell or leaf were somehow expanding.

3. Next, visualize a pathway from your palms through your wrists to your elbows and up to your shoulders, then down to your heart. See this as a channel for information from your chosen find. If you were to draw this channel, it would be a heart shape – the bottom point of your clasped hands making two arcs with your elbows and shoulders and finishing at the heart. Visualize this shape, feeling the object's vibration running through you.

4. Pay attention to how this vibration feels. You'll now sense that your first physical impressions through touch are being translated: the roughness of a root gives you a feeling of rootedness and balance. The coldness of a shell now feels as if there's something warm and soft inside. Whatever impressions you receive through touch, give your found object a meaning that's personal to you, at this moment.

Your body, rather than your mind, will often respond to the information coming through the heart pathway in this ritual. You may experience a faint buzz or tingle on your skin, a sense of activity around your heart, a tiny flip in your solar plexus. A physical reaction is confirmation that you're attuned to and connected with your charm.

WORKING AT A DISTANCE

If you don't wish to hold your object, or you'd simply like to "read" a plant or other object in situ, you can practise the ritual above at a distance.

Sit or stand as close to the object as you comfortably can, with your palms loosely crossed on your lap or at waist height, so you're making the shape of the heart pathway. As above, sense if you're welcome to connect, and if you feel at home here, begin. Visualize the heart pathway and invite your find to connect with you through your palms.

SENSING SPIRIT WITH THE THIRD EYE

We use the breath to connect with the energy field or aura of a plant or mineral. Once connected, you may "see" this energy as colour or feel a colour or shape internally. Sensing the aura connects you to the object's *deva* or spirit. The deeper your connection with the spirit of your chosen find, the more you empower it to work with and for you.

This works best when you're at a distance from your object. The distance depends on the size of your find – a piece of wood about a hand high should be about an arm's length away from you. If you have a small pebble, for example, bring it to around a palm-length away. Create the distance you need for a comfortable focus.

TECHNIQUE
Connecting with Your
Find's Energy Field

1. Sit comfortably and touch the earth. This gesture asks that you remain grounded and in your body during this practice.
2. Close your eyes and visualize that you're drawing energy from the earth up through the centre of your body into your solar plexus. The solar plexus chakra (energy centre) is associated with self-knowledge and soul wisdom.
3. Match this image with a physical action – a deep in-breath. Hold for a second or two, then exhale. If you can, imagine your solar plexus area is glowing yellow; it's your inner sun, burning with solar power.
4. Next, take a second, deep in-breath, and exhale as you bring energy up from the solar plexus to your heart chakra, which is glowing pink, and feel the warmth of love. Breathe in again, bringing the energy up to the third eye chakra (between the eyebrows), and breathe out as you focus your attention on your third eye, which is your "intuition point".

5. Breathe naturally and sense the colour purple or white around your third eye. Feel that you're sending these colours outward toward your charm. You're extending your energy field and heightening your senses. It's the feeling you get when you're standing tall, with your arms open and head lifted – as if opening up your whole self.

Now you have activated your solar plexus, heart and third-eye chakras, you are ready to receive sensory information from your chosen charm.

1. Half-open your eyes and gaze at your find. You may prefer to turn your head sideways and use your peripheral vision. Do this until you need to blink, then close your eyes, taking the memory of the object with you. What do you see?
2. After a few moments, look again at the object and repeat. You may sense a colour around your find or see it in your mind's eye. You may hear the name of the colour as a whisper.
3. Reflect on the colours or quality of the energy field you sense. You don't need to attribute meaning to particular colours; just focus on what you feel – for example, if the sense of the colour is vibrant, muted, pale or gentle.
4. Be open to what follows. You may find that you're sensing the object's history – if a plant, perhaps how it was once used medicinally, a knowing about its healing properties. From a stone you may sense how far it's travelled. This is the object's spirit or *deva* speaking.
5. When you are ready, open your eyes fully, take a few deep breaths, and touch the earth to affirm that you're grounded.

As we are all different, we will experience our find's energy field in our own way. For example, when I observe or hold wild mint, I instantly feel that the plant's aura is violet, seeing the colour internally rather than literally around the plant's form. However, some people don't see auric colours, but sense the quality of the aura as sharp squiggles or as a smooth, even line.

"The way we respond to nature is unique, and there are many shades of approach."

Making a connection with a find can take as much or as little time as you choose. You may work through each stage of connection – from observation to reading an object through touch or at a distance. Alternatively, just one reading technique may feel right for you. The way we respond to nature is unique, and there are many shades of approach.

TECHNIQUE
Making and Dedicating
Your First Charm

Making Your First Charm

First, decide if you'd like your charm to be singular – say, one stone or one shell – or if you want your charm to comprise two or more items together.

If you want to tie two items together, make sure you have your dedication ready, as you will recite the dedication as you bind them and finish with a knot. Some charms may fit together naturally and not need to be tied, such as a small stone that fits into a nutshell or a feather into a tubular reed. However, you can still bind them together as part of the ritual of dedication. If you have a singular charm, you can wrap it in a length of thread and tie it as a reminder of your wish for it to help you.

To tie a charm, you'll need some vine or strong grass, or thread, braid, cord, wool, ribbon, raffia or string. Vine or strong grass can be harder to work with as they can be tough or a little brittle, so you may feel more comfortable using thread or string for your first charm.

You can make your charm at home or out in nature if the weather is fine and it's not too breezy. Making your charm outdoors as part of your walk may feel easier than indoors, because you'll already have a relaxed, creative mindset.

Dedicating Your Charm

Dedicating an object as a charm is to formalize its purpose. You've already sensed what your charm may do – it may feel protective, loving or calming. The next step is to give your charm a unique mission. If, for example, you had a black-and-white pebble, you might ask it to help you make decisions. If it's a small, delicate flower, you may wish to dedicate it to supporting relationships. Match the qualities with the intention and you'll have a charm that empowers your wishes.

To dedicate your charm:
- Hold it in your palm.
- Ask it to work with you.
- If you you're binding your charm, begin to do this as you say aloud:

  "I dedicate this charm to …" [name the purpose or wish]
- Repeat twice, so you say the dedication three times. Three is a dynamic number in charm-work (see page 212).
- Finish with, "So mote it be" as you tie the knot to secure your thread or string. Alternatively, you can say, "Amen," or "Let this be done," or a similar phrase that's right for you.

You can also draw upon existing plant and mineral lore when choosing your finds. For example, you might choose to work with an oak leaf – for wisdom – along with a small black stone you've dedicated for protection; together, the oak leaf and the stone act as a charm to ward off doubt and connect to higher guidance.

RITUAL
A Charm for Immediate Help

If you have an issue to deal with in the coming days, you can dedicate your charm (see above) to help you. For example, your overriding need might be for protection if you're about to be launched into a situation you feel you have little control over. You may go for "an inspired solution" or "efficiency" if you're overwhelmed with demands on your time, and so on.

Here are some examples of when you can use your charm, though you may wish to think up your own purposes too.

A charm can help you:

- Protect your personal boundaries
- Make decisions
- Reduce stress at work
- Travel safely
- Increase efficiency
- Let go of anxiety or anger
- Find an inspired solution.

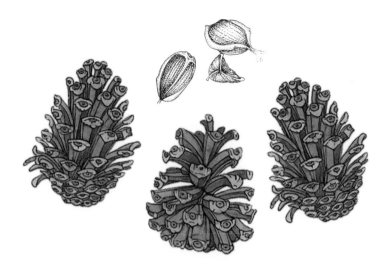

It's best to choose one thing you'd like your charm to do and focus on one specific issue, as this intensifies the energy of your intention. When you have decided, simply follow the steps outlined on pages 46–47 to dedicate your charm.

Remember though that here, in nature, you're already taking the medicine for whatever challenges you'll meet over the next few days or weeks. The feeling of centredness and oneness gives you space to begin working on the issue at an unconscious level. As you dedicate your charm to your purpose, you may find you get a "flash insight" showing you how best to approach the situation you're thinking of.

Carry your charm with you or place it on your altar (see pages 57–63) for up to seven days if it's delicate, and longer if made from resilient matter such as stones, pine cones, feathers, nutshells, twigs and bark. When your situation has resolved and you no longer need your charm, give gratitude for its work and return it to the earth.

RECEIVING INTUITIVE INSIGHTS

The sensory experience of a nature walk – the heightened awareness we feel as we tune in to the environment – can bring intuitive impressions, or flashes. Intuition can be seen as the synthesis, or outcome, of the sensory information we're silently processing as we walk. This processing happens beneath the radar of our awareness, so when an intuitive flash comes to the surface it feels sudden, unexpected – like a fish flipping up from still waters.

Intuition has been described as a leap of consciousness. If we see nature as existing at a level of consciousness that is different from human consciousness, intuition can act as a bridge between our two worlds.

THE *GENIUS LOCI* – SPIRITS OF THE LAND

As you do more charm-walking you'll become more sensitive, not only to the detail of your personal finds, but to the land and its inhabitants. You'll sense the energetic signatures wherever you walk, which change subtly with every step. One place in nature can feel very different to another, even in the smallest ways. It can be practical – resting in a dip feels more sheltered and private, but there's even more going on. How many times have you sat in the "ideal" place, then moved? More than once? Where you sit or stand in nature for any time has to feel right. You need to feel rooted, safe, peaceful. What you're doing, unknowingly, is connecting with the spirits of the place, or *genius loci*, and using that sense to find a place that is uniquely right for you.

The concept of land or place spirits is found in the stories of indwelling spirits, who may be benevolent or dreadful, symbols of nature's light and shade, its abundance or dangerous enchantment. In Greek mythology, feminine nature-spirits, known as nymphs, dwelled in trees, waterfalls, rivers, lakes, valleys and mountains. Wood-nymphs were often named after the trees they protected, such as the Daphnaie ("laurel") or the beautiful Leuce ("white goddess", who lived in the white poplar). Rarely glimpsed by the human eye, nymphs came out to dance only when all was quiet in the forest.

In Romanian mythology, the *balour* or waterman lurked in deep water, waiting to lure unfortunate travellers to their deaths. The belief in water-gods threads through many ancient cultures, in the ritual tying of cloth to trees guarding sacred springs (page 85) and dropping pennies into wishing wells to appease the gods while travelling through their land.

Other protective charms were used, too, such as carrying a piece of wood from the lime or linden wood to ward off Gana, Romanian queen of the witches, the enchantress who led the wild hunt over heaven earth.

The magical aspect of the land, and particularly the forest, gives us many gods and lesser deities, from Tapio, protector-god of the forest in Finnish mythology, to the *ghillie due*, the Scottish male fairy who dwelled in a grove of birch trees and guided people who had lost their way. Standing stones, too, were thought to have certain powers – *Lia Fail*, Ireland's Stone of Destiny, could shriek in protest or roar with joy.

The tales of these deities were often seen as containing guidelines for how to travel the land, and the importance of respecting and appreciating nature's power, danger and beauty.

RESTORING BALANCE TO THE LAND

As you walk, tune in to the subtle currents of place, sensing the changes as you go from field to stream, hillside to woodland. If you sense that an area is unwelcoming, you can offer up a gift. Making an offering to a place that feels drained or negative signifies your positive intention to restore balance. You could leave one of your charms there or look for a new charm to leave on this land, maybe a small bundle of herbs tied with grass, or a feather or a single wild flower. When you've placed your gift, quietly move away.

WORKING WITH A PENDULUM

A pendulum – a weight suspended from a chain – is used in divination to receive answers to questions. It's also used to divine the location of underground water and other hidden minerals, as it's believed to respond to the changing vibration of the earth. Working with a pendulum is also a way to connect with the spirits of the land, to sense information about its history.

The simplest pendulum to make is perhaps using a hag stone (also known as a witch or fairy stone, or a holey stone because it has a hole all the way through it – pages 149–150), which you thread with a length of long grass, cord or thread.

At a recent nature charms workshop, I asked participants to meander around an extensive garden and take a little from whichever plant they chose. One person returned saying she'd been rejected: she had wanted to take a leaf or two from a wild strawberry plant, but felt she was being sent away. The area she had chosen was a quiet corner by the compost heap, so she'd wanted to give it some attention. On relating this to the group, others agreed. It's interesting how people naturally wanted to connect with this part of the garden – they said, "It felt unloved". I went to that area of the garden alone, later, to investigate. Using a pendulum, I asked questions, divining that the spirit of that area of the garden did not want strawberries growing there. I later discovered that the strawberry beds had been a recent addition to the garden, before we moved in. The strawberries never bore much fruit.

TECHNIQUE
Tuning in to Your Pendulum

1. Attune to the hag stone by holding it (see pages 149–150), then hold it vertically, so it's able to swing.
2. Close your eyes and sense how the pendulum begins to tremble or move a little. Then, open your eyes.
3. You will need to know which way means "yes" and which way "no", so start by asking a simple question. Ask, "Is my name X?" speaking your name, and it will move – swinging back and forward or circling. As you know this to be true, this is your "yes" position.
4. Repeat the question this time with an incorrect name, and you'll see the pendulum's movement for "no". For example, you may get the pendulum moving in a diagonal line for "no" and a clockwise motion for "yes".

Once you know your "yes" and "no" positions, you're ready to use your pendulum.

RITUAL
Connecting with the Spirits of the Land

Start by holding your pendulum in your dominant hand. Ask if you can make a connection and see if the pendulum swings "yes "or "no". If the answer is uncertain, for example if your pendulum trembles but doesn't move, take this as "no", and move on to another spot. If you're concerned that you may be influencing the pendulum's movement, ask your question with your eyes closed and only open them after the movement has begun.

"Your pendulum might guide you to ley lines – an ancient energy matrix that runs between historical places."

When you have a "yes" response, close your eyes and take a breath. What do you feel about this place? Images or words that describe this may come to you. Then, ask the pendulum about your impressions. You may feel this has been a sacred place; if so, ask the spirits through the pendulum. You might have a knowing that the land was once agricultural, or sense that a tree nearby has a special significance. If you're by a river, you could call upon the river spirit.

Your pendulum might also guide you to ley lines – an ancient energy matrix that runs between historical places – by becoming very active where the ley line is located. You'll feel the change in the vibration and movement of your pendulum as you walk the land.

When you have finished communing with the *genius loci*, thank this spirit for working with you.

It's fine, too, if you don't sense the land-spirits; this ability often comes with familiarity, when taking a sensory walk becomes second nature. Until then, think of the pendulum as a way to focus your attention. Whether you choose to ask questions or not, simply feeling the movement of the pendulum and observing it is a calming practice that helps you feel settled and linked to the environment, right here, right now.

CARRYING AND WEARING CHARMS

You can carry your charm with you on your person whenever you need its help. Keep your charm in a pocket or purse; wear it as a pendant, as for herb pouches (see pages 118–119) or hag stones (see pages 149–150), or as a brooch, pinned to your clothing. How you carry your charm depends on what it's made from – fresh leaves tucked away in a pocket for too long may turn to a pulp, while small sprigs of fresh herb in a pouch worn as a pendant will keep their form, as they'll be aerated.

You can keep your charm as long as it lasts and feels right. If your charm is fragile and breaks, or when you sense a plant charm, for example, has done its work, return it to the earth with gratitude. A plant charm keeps for up to a week, but there's no need to discard it if you love it and it's still working for you. If you have charms of stone, shell and feather, for example, you may choose to wear or otherwise keep them for many months or years to come – but again, when you feel you don't need your charm anymore, let it go. You may decide to wear or carry some charms for a long time because of the feeling they give you when you hold them. Stones become imprinted with your energy, and you may feel very attached for a period of time, then decide to set it aside until you feel drawn to carry it again.

PRESERVING CHARMS

To help your "green" finds last, you can spray them with acrylic or use glycerine or PVA glue. For information on how to press leaves and flowers, see page 122.

Acrylic spray: Using acrylic spray is great for preserving delicate or spherical charms, such as seed heads and flower heads. The spray hardens a plant's surfaces, preserving its colour and preventing deterioration. Look out for eco-friendly sprays containing alcohol made from sugar cane rather than petroleum-based solvent.

Take your finds into your garden, yard or a well-ventilated space. Position them upright – prop them in an old vase or tie them to a piece of thread and hang them. Alternatively, use tongs to hold them while spraying, or spray them face-down on newspaper. Wearing a mask, spray from the distance given on the canister and leave your finds to dry.

Glycerine and craft glue: This method works well for leaves, as it brings out the richness of their natural colours. To use glycerine, take a dish or pan and add 250ml (9fl oz) vegetable glycerine with 1 litre (35fl oz) water and stir. Submerge the leaves in the liquid for around four days, then remove and blot with paper towel. To use craft glue (PVA), coat one side of the leaves with the glue using a brush. The glue goes on white but dries clear. When dry, turn over the leaves and repeat.

Electroforming: If you're really ambitious, get hold of an electroforming kit, which plates non-metallic objects with metal, turning your leaves, acorns, cones or shells to brilliant gold, silver or copper.

MAKING AN ALTAR AT HOME

Placing your charms in a dedicated space is a time-old way to honour what you value and what you hope for, from making wishes and requests to deities to calling upon ancestors for guidance. For some people, a personal altar is an expression of a belief system, particularly in Pagan and Wiccan traditions. You can start your altar by including some of the following objects to represent the four elements:

Earth elements
- Crystals
- Bottled sand
- Bowl of garden soil

Air elements
- Incense
- Smudge stick
- Candles (both fire and air), but be sure to keep any flammable charms well away

Fire elements
- Candles (both fire and air)
- Aromatherapy burner (both fire and water)

Water elements
- Seashells
- Sea salt
- A small bowl of water with crystals
- Bottled sea water

Think about where you'd like to put your charms. You can place them alongside their element – so if you have crystals on your altar (earth),

TECHNIQUE
How to Make Your Altar

1. Choose a small table, cabinet top, dresser, shelf or any suitable surface in a quiet part of your home where you can sit comfortably.
2. Cover it with a cloth to mark it as your designated sacred space (you can shake out the cloth easily when you're ready to replace items or start anew).
3. To begin with, choose objects that represent the four elements: earth, air, fire and water; then add your charms. The elements evoke nature and give your charm a natural setting, which can energize and empower it.

you might position a stone charm (earth element) next to it; a feather charm would go with an air item, close to incense, for example. Or simply place your charms wherever they sit right – there are no rules, just an opportunity to get creative. The kitchen's also a great source of altar ingredients. When you have your four elements and charms in place, you might add herbs and spices, such as pretty star anise, cinnamon cones, peppercorns, cardamom pods and more.

"Making a nature altar is a beautiful
way to celebrate what the natural
world means to you."

Earth charms

- Stones
- Leaves (can also represent air)
- Flowers and petals
- Bark
- Pine cones, nut shells, seeds

Air charms

- Feathers
- Leaves (can also represent earth)

Fire charms

- Twigs and small branches

Water charms

- Seashells
- Seaweed
- Seashore pebbles

Making a nature altar is a beautiful way to celebrate what the natural world means to you. Once you have chosen the objects to represent the elements, you can start placing your charms on your altar. This is a powerful visual reminder of the hopes and wishes your charms represent. And rather than carry a charm, you may prefer to set it on your altar and give it your attention for a little time each day. You may also like to meditate at your nature altar (see opposite) or just spend a minute or two reminding yourself of your connection to the natural world, particularly when you can't get outdoors.

A ONE-ELEMENT ALTAR

If you prefer, you can dedicate your altar to one sole element, according to what you wish for:

Earth: Material needs, such as money, wellbeing and security
Air: Ideas and spiritual connection
Fire: Energy, protection and passion
Water: Creativity and relationships

You can bring in colour to represent the element of your choice, too: greens and browns for earth; purple and metallics for air; red and oranges for fire; and blues for water. Naturally, go with your own colour associations, too.

TECHNIQUE
Meditating at Your Altar

An altar gives you a set space for meditation practice; regular meditation – even just a few minutes each day – gives you time to clear your mind, de-stress and connect with your inner knowing.

1. Begin by lighting incense, a candle or aromatherapy burner to signal the start of your practice.
2. Get comfortable, take a deep breath or two, and turn your gaze to one of your altar charms.
3. Half-close your eyes, keeping your gaze on your charm. Focus on your gentle breathing, feeling your breath flowing through your body. Visualize that you're breathing in white light. When

you exhale, you are breathing out whatever you do not need in your life just now – stress, anxious thoughts, to-do lists. Do this letting-go until you sense a shift: a softening in your body and fewer thoughts running through your mind.

4. Let your eyes close and sense the stillness within you. Pay attention to how you feel by noticing the sensations in your body, rather than the thoughts in your head. There is nothing to think about.

5. It's natural for the chatter of our minds to interrupt. Whenever this happens, half-open your eyes and look again at your charm; it acts as an anchor during your meditation, bringing you back to stillness. Close your eyes again, and go on with your meditation.

6. Continue for as long as it feels right.

7. Gently open your eyes and return to the everyday world.

8. When you have finished, extinguish the candle, incense or burner.

RITUAL
Manifesting with Your Altar Charms

The time between a new moon and a full moon is associated with growth – when the moon is growing to fullness. The waning phase of the moon is linked with release. Meditating on a charm and a wish at the time of a new moon strengthens your existing intention for your charm, giving your desire an energy boost.

1. Follow the basic meditation technique on page 61, this time holding your charm.

2. When you find space and peace within, declare your request and visualize the ideal outcome. For example:

   a. If you want help beginning a new project, meditate with your charm on a new moon, and imagine your idea taking root.

   b. To grow an existing project or if you wish for a relationship to develop, meditate with your charm during a waxing moon phase – between a new moon and full moon.

   c. To release an old situation, meditate during the waning moon. In your mind's eye see that issue vanishing, as you hold your charm and it supports your wish.

4. When you have finished, give thanks, replace your charm on your altar and extinguish your candle.

REFRESHING YOUR ALTAR

When any plant matter on your altar becomes limp or faded, return it to the earth with thanks. You may decide you love your faded rose petals or dry twigs, though – if so, keep them for as long as you choose.

Tidy and refresh your altar every week, removing any charm debris, and adding in new items to keep the energy of this special space alive. It's also worth keeping a record of your altars, so take photographs or write down and/or sketch your arrangements to preserve the memory of your creations and your wishes.

THE CHARM TREE

A charm tree is a symbol of growth and hope. As with an altar, it gathers pieces found on your walks in one place, and offers a special space for reflection, meditation and manifesting. If you follow moon cycles, a good time to set up your tree is on a new moon, as this is a time of increase when it's auspicious to make wishes. Make a charm tree to celebrate special times: Samhain, Hallowe'en, Yule, Thanksgiving, the equinoxes. Otherwise, you can dedicate your tree to gratitude, love, forgiveness, creativity or any other positive quality.

TECHNIQUE
Making a Charm Tree

All you need are a few fallen branches or some driftwood.

1. Look for wood with lots of offshoots and gnarls – these will act as hooks for your hanging charms, so they won't skitter down the branches.
2. Let the wood dry out for a few days, then arrange the branches in a basket, jar or pot.
3. Hold the branches in position, by packing the container with stones, moss or any other filler material (I use short lengths of dry reed from a garden plant).
4. Choose your charms and arrange them on your tree.

Charms to thread or tie on a charm tree include:

- Cones
- Feathers
- Shells with holes
- Knot charms (see pages 135–137)
- Hag stones (see pages 149–150)
- Vine bracelets (see pages 138–139)
- Wishes written on luggage ties or fabric strips (see clootie trees, pages 85–87).

Keep the tree vibrant by adding fresh finds from your walks every week. On a new moon, re-set your tree by changing or moving the charms around. Write new wishes and set new goals.

FOLLOWING NATURE'S COMPASS

Letting your intuition guide you in nature helps immerse you in the natural world. In the next ritual, you follow your natural attraction to a charm, then let it lead you in turn to another find. In this way, you let your charms direct you from one place to another – an intuitive compass, taking you where you need to go. You can physically carry a charm from place to place, or do this ritual without touch by gazing and connecting with a fallen object, plant or tree.

"By following your intuitive response rather than complying with the 'ideal' visitor experience of the land, you'll find your outings more rewarding because your walk becomes more personal to you."

Vast, open landscapes can feel overwhelming, whether you're venturing into wild moorland or a country park. You may feel a pressure to try to see it all and do everything on offer – whether following suggested pathways or routes or completing that recommended three-mile circular walk. When you use nature's charms as a compass, you might find you're drawn to explore just a small part of a bigger landscape because this is what you need today. By following your intuitive response rather than complying with the "ideal" visitor experience of the land, you'll find your outings more rewarding because your walk becomes more personal to you. It doesn't have to take much time, either – if you have just 30 minutes in a local park rather than a day to spend in the countryside, that's fine.

TECHNIQUE
The Charm Compass

Start by following the suggestions on pages 30–34 on approaching nature – beginning with gratitude, opening your senses and seeing what naturally attracts you. Then, choose one find, and gaze at it or hold it to make a connection by tuning into its energy field.

Sense where you need to go next, and let your body tell you through subtle movement. You may feel a gentle pull forward, sideways or behind you. Or you might be guided by the shape or character of your find – for example, a tip of a feather pointing east or an arrow shape in fallen bark.

Carrying your find with you, go in that direction, and walk on to see what next catches your eye. When you reach find number two, put down the first find.

Now pick up find number two and repeat this as many times as you wish, each time sensing where your body wants to go. You'll start to see the objects on your walk as signposts guiding you through the areas that your heart, rather than your head, wants you to visit.

When you repeat this again in the same park, beach, meadow or woodland, you may follow a similar trail each time, and the trees and plants you meet become familiar friends.

Other times, your intuitive compass may lead you to explore new areas and make new connections with the land. Each time you go out, you'll find something that reflects what you need at that moment in time.

If you prefer not to pick up your finds, you can enjoy this treasure hunt through gaze rather than touch. When you come to an area, plant or other material you're drawn to, spend a few moments observing and connecting, then sense where you naturally want to go next.

If you don't take any finds, you can photograph them on your phone as a visual reminder of your experience. Having photos of the finds you're drawn to keeps you connected to nature when you can't be there.

Wandering with a Friend

If you enjoy company on your walks, this technique is perfect for sharing. When wandering with a friend, agree to describe what you feel and see as you go. When you talk in the present tense (rather than relating what happened earlier in the past tense), you make your experience real.

Speaking transforms thought into reality, and as you talk, you feel a shift in energy. You'll also discover you make further connections that emerge as you speak – and ideas develop as you weave your observations into sentences.

It may feel difficult to express everything you sense and feel, but try giving your impressions a voice. It's particularly helpful to do this if you're drifting into mental to-do lists and worries, and you start to feel disconnected from the environment. Verbalizing what you notice and why anchors you in the present, peaceful moment.

You may prefer to begin a walk with company, or go your own way then meet up afterwards to talk about your experiences (even if you'd like to walk together, your intuitive compasses may take you in different directions). If so, agree a time and a meeting place at the end of your walk.

NOTICING SYMBOLS: REFLECTION

When you come to the end of your journey, or at home afterwards, make time for reflection. Think about the finds that led you on a trail and ask yourself if there were any similarities. Maybe you were drawn mainly to trees or stones, or perhaps textures – the roughness of an ear of grass or the feel of a dry leaf crumbling in your fingers? You may have noticed certain shapes or symbols recurring, too (see Chapter 10). It can be useful to draw or write about your intuitive nature walk, noting the symbols and patterns you saw. As you recall your experience, more images and ideas will arise.

PART TWO

Natural Charms

In this part, we discover how to make charms from any treasure found on our walks, from herbs and feathers to shells and seaweed. In each section, myth and folklore are presented as a way to understand why certain charms mean what they do, and as a basis for showing us how to develop our own meanings and relationships with the charms we find in our area.

3

Trees

Growth and Transformation

Most trees represent wisdom, protection and luck, their meanings stemming from trees' physical strength and longevity. A tree's ability to deliver shelter, wood for fire and fruits for sustenance naturally aligns the tree with protection and good fortune. Given our ancestors' deep reliance on trees for survival, in many cultures trees were, and are still, deified. An evolving pantheon of gods, goddesses and lesser deities walk among our groves and forests, their spirits and stories intimately bound to wood.

> "The relationship between tree and deity, man and magic, may explain the connection between trees and divination."

In this sense, trees are imbued with magic – the wood, sacred; rustling leaves, the god speaking. According to myth, the Nordic god, Odin, hung from the world tree, an ash and the symbol of immortality, for nine days and nights, gaining the gift of prophesy. In psychology, the forest is the symbol of the unconscious, the mysteries of the self. Traditionally, in European folklore, we have magic wands from nut-bearing trees and witches' broomsticks of hawthorn and hazelwood; in rural practice, V- or Y-shaped branches made from hazel or willow trees could, as if by magic, lead a person to water. This relationship between tree and deity, man and magic, may also explain the connection between trees and divination. Runes – an alphabet of angular letters used by ancient Germanic peoples from the first or second century CE – were carved from fruit-bearing trees and cast to divine the outcome of a journey or battle; and fruit stones, such as apple pips were cast in divination rituals to call upon the gods for answers to questions.

HUMAN AND DIVINE

Symbolically, the tree stands for fertility, the cycle of the seasons and the interconnectedness of life, as well as longevity. The world tree or cosmic tree is a central motif in many mythologies, which in early cultures explained our human relationship with the celestial realms. The branches uphold the heavens – which may be why birds are seen as spiritual messengers, flitting between sky and branch – while the roots represent the underworld and the ancestors; and the trunk connects the two, a pathway from earth to heaven. The figure of the tree is closely tied to the human form, too, with feet as roots, the body as trunk, and raised arms and hands as branches and leaves. Given that deities take human form, this physical echo of ourselves or our gods as trees makes the natural connection between us all the deeper.

Knocking on wood for luck probably comes from the ancient tradition of asking the indwelling deity in a tree for help – one knock was the request, and the second knock was the "thank you". In the UK, "touch wood" is an expression said for protection from bad luck, or to ask for a run of good luck to continue.

The acceptance of an indwelling deity gives trees protection or protects humans from harm. Many trees are considered sacred, which prevents them being destroyed, and lesser trees had their own keepers, who guarded them from damage and destruction. Danish folklore tells how the elder tree housed a dryad, or tree spirit called Hyle-Moer, or Elder-Tree Mother who protected the elder. If anyone felled an elder for furniture, the dryad would follow the wood to its new home and haunt the owners to avenge the tree's destruction.

In northern English lore, Yorkshire superstition has it that the tree-fairies Churn Milk Peg and Melch Dick hide in nut trees and bushes, pinching those who try to take unripe nuts ("churn milk" refers to unripe nut pulp, and "melch" means unripe, too). This tale deterred children from eating unripe nuts and having stomach upsets, but, as ever, there's often a darker side to the faerie folk. The tale continues: when a group of boys takes a hoard of hazelnuts and almonds from the woods one night, Melch Dick takes Doed, the smallest of the boys to a pool under moonlight, overhung with a ring of aspen trees. He tries to bewitch Doed and turn him into a squirrel. By reciting the prayer, "Matthew, Mark, Luke and John, Bless the bed that I lay on", the boy breaks the spell and finally escapes – his lesson learned.

PROTECTION: WARDEN TREES

Some trees are said to protect the home – this was often an old, substantial tree growing near the house, which guarded against bad spirits and bad luck. In Sweden, linden (lime) trees gave rise to the popular surname of Lind. In the English county of Herefordshire, small crosses of birch and rowan trees were placed above the doors of houses on May Day for luck and to protect residents against the spells of witches, who were thought to be particularly active at that time of year (and who often got the blame for any type of natural misfortune). A bay tree set either side of a front door was also believed to ward off bad luck. The Irish tale *The Settling of the Manor of Tara*, set in the first century, tells how a giant came to Tara, the ancient capital of Ireland, from Lebanon with a magical branch bearing hazelnuts, apples and edible acorns. The fruit became the five sacred trees of Ireland that would each guard one of the country's five provinces. But the giant spoke a prophecy, too – that the trees would protect the king and his tribe but would fall when Christianity drove out Paganism. These five trees comprised three ash and two yew, including the Tree of Ross, a yew described as a "firm straight deity".[11] According to the English poet Robert Graves, one yew tree may in fact have been blackthorn. In all, the trees spelled out the prophecy: yew for death, ash for battle (as it was used to make bows and the shafts of weapons) and blackthorn for disruption.

FERTILITY AND HEALING

Fruit- and nut-bearing trees are naturally associated with fertility and good health. In Baltic folklore, Laima, the goddess of fate and childbirth, appeared in the linden tree in the form of a cuckoo. Women went to the linden tree to ask her for luck and the blessings of fertility, leaving offerings in return.

In southern England, villagers ritually poured cider over the roots of an apple tree to ensure a bountiful apple crop in the coming year. They bowed down to the tree as if burdened by a heavy load of fruit, and the men shot guns to drive away bad spirits. The villagers wassailed and sang to invoke a plentiful yield. One version of the song goes:

"Bud well, bear well
God send you fare well;
Every sprig and every spray
A bushel of apples next New Year Day."

A similar tale involved appeasing the Apple Tree Man, the spirit who lived in the oldest apple tree in the orchard. In one rendering of the tale, the Apple Tree Man rewards a man who offered the orchard his last cup of cider by showing him where to find buried gold.

Our intrinsic dependency on trees makes for some fascinating lore, in which there can be a fateful bond between tree and human. If a child became ill, trees such as the ash, oak or willow were split to signify the illness, then the child was passed through the cleft three or nine times. The tree was then bound up and its wound anointed with clay or mud to symbolize the healing. If the split in the tree didn't heal or the tree died, that too would be the child's fate.

> "In European folklore, the willow tree was a keeper of secrets: tell a secret to the willow and it will stay safe inside its trunk."

WOOD AND BRANCH CHARMS

As virtually every tree at some time has been associated with strength, protection, fertility, magic and the power to heal, there's much anecdotal evidence of branches and twigs as charms. In Druid tradition, the thunder-struck oak's mistletoe was a sacred charm of prophesy. In European folklore, the willow tree was a keeper of secrets: tell a secret to the willow and it will stay safe inside its trunk.

Hazel and holly, among many others, are luck-bringers (finding a holly sprig predicted unexpected good luck), and poplar was a sign of money. Wearing birch twigs on your hat or in your buttonhole brought good fortune and warded off the evil eye. In Bempton, Yorkshire, a forked piece of rowan wood was carried for protection. In Cameroon, the Bamum and Bamileke peoples, according to Jean Chevalier and Alain Gheerbrant, "have a chip of bamboo which they call a *guis* ('laugh'), which is their symbol of happiness, the unadorned happiness of a life free from illness and care."[12]

This glimpse into tree lore is your foundation, rather than a set of rules: the aim is to work with any tree charm you choose and ask it to work for you. As folklore is often localized (relevant to the trees that grow in particular counties or countries) you can work with the trees common to your area. And you can divine the properties of those trees by communicating with your chosen tree even before you pick up a charm.

Tree Charm Examples

Bark, twigs, pieces of branch, root pieces, leaves, buds. (For fruits, nuts, seeds and berries, see page 106.)

TECHNIQUE
Finding Your Charm Tree

When you first walk among trees, open your senses by switching your focus from your thoughts to what your senses are telling you. This will bring you into the present moment. Wander toward a tree, slowly, then pause. Make a connection to the tree with your breath (see pages 43–44) – remember we use the breath to connect with the energy field or aura of a tree or mineral and this may enable you to "see" the tree's aura as a colour or feel a colour or shape.

1. Ask permission from the tree to come closer and to touch it. You will sense it replying "yes" or "no", and feel the answer physically as a gentle pull in your body toward or away from your tree. If the answer is "yes", step under the canopy of branches.

2. At first, be the observer. Look down toward the roots, then at the trunk, then skyward. Take in any unusual patterns, such as whorls in the bark or any intricate weave of surface roots. Tune in to the tree's sound – listen to its branches creaking, its leaves rustling. There may be silence. Gathering sensory impressions tunes you into the tree's energy frequency.

3. Sit or stand with your back against the trunk. Wait and listen, feeling the subtle vibrations. Let go of any expectations and immerse yourself in this sacred space to see what arises. Patience is important; you may need to spend some time here, simply being with yourself and your tree, accepting it exactly as it stands. Trees communicate on their terms, when the time is right, and you may need to build up a relationship with your tree over several visits before you begin to sense what it has to say.

4. You may feel the tree's message as a knowing, which you hear in words or see in internal imagery. This part of the process is imaginative, as you're naturally interpreting what you sense. For instance, you may have a flash memory of scraping your knee as a child and associate the tree with healing or dealing with a past wound. Or, as you sit against your tree you may feel a deep serenity, so you associate your tree with feeling calm and safe. Perhaps you hear a phrase in your mind that advises you how to address a problem, and so you feel your tree is an illuminator, helping you unearth your own solutions.

5. When you feel ready, look for finds beneath your tree – fallen leaves, bark, small branches, broken root, twigs, cones, nuts and nutshells, fruit or seeds. Spend just a few minutes doing this. You can either commune with each of these items and return them where you found them, or dedicate them as charms to take away. When you have finished, give thanks to the tree before you leave.

TREE RITUAL
Charm for Completion

As the tree represents the whole of the universe, a tree charm made from items representing the roots, trunk and branches symbolizes a wish for wholeness. As you gather and put together your charm items, reflect on how you can accept your situation just as it is, and for that to be perfect. When something is fully accepted, it becomes complete – and is no longer an issue. Any feelings of lack dissolve and balance returns.

Gather one item to represent the past, one for the present and one for the future. You can also have your three items signify the mind, body and spirit, if you prefer, or the unconscious, the conscious mind and universal consciousness.

The past: Roots, a dry or autumnal leaf, a nutshell, a pine cone, an ash or sycamore seed

The present: Bark, a fresh leaf

The future: Fruit pips, berries, fruit (if safe to touch), buds, a small twig

Bind your three finds together as one charm using long grass, cord or thread, finishing with one knot to seal in your wish. As you make your charm, set your intention to solve your problem, restore balance or find forgiveness and acceptance – whatever is needed.

Keep your charm for around seven days, or until you feel its work is done. You can carry it around with you or display it on your altar.

TREE RITUAL
The "Airt o' the Clicky"

John MacTaggart, in his *Scottish Gallovidian Encyclopedia*, says, "When a pilgrim at any time gets bewildered, he poises his staff perpendicular on the way, then leaves it to itself, and on whatever direction it falls, and that he pursues." This superstition was known as the "airt o' the clicky", or the direction of the staff. MacTaggart also observed that those who used the clicky this way "mostly cause it to gravitate toward the place they have a secret inclination to go to". When you're walking, find a straightish branch, put one end on the ground and then let it fall like the clicky. Follow the direction in which it points and discover where your inner compass wants you to go next.

"CLOOTIE" TREE OFFERINGS AND WISHING TREES

A "clootie" is a Scottish term for a tree that grows by a sacred well or a spring famed for its healing waters. These trees are seen as magical, and in early Celtic cultures people made pilgrimages to clootie trees to leave offerings and ask for healing from the tree's deity, goddess or spirit – such as the Celtic deity Brigit, who was associated with sacred springs and wells. These requests took the form of rags tied to branches (*clooti* is a Scottish word for cloth). And as the cloth faded and eventually perished, so would the ailment in an act of sympathetic magic.

"New wishing trees have recently been established in many parts of the world, with visitors hanging paper, fabric, trinkets and ribbons."

The sister of the clootie is the wishing tree – a tree often decorated with rags, ribbons or coins to represent wishes – and many continue to thrive today. In County Meath, Ireland, stands a hawthorn wishing tree adorned with ribbons; in Japan, people celebrate the Star Festival on 7 July by adorning bamboo plants with wishes written on paper strips. Then, there are the coin or money trees – old, felled trees into which visitors hammer coins for luck and healing. They're studded with hundreds of coins, some dating from centuries ago. In rural Arkansas, young women once tied scraps of old cloth to the branches of trees such as the hawthorn, pawpaw and ironwood, to wish for love. New wishing trees have recently been established, too, in many parts of the world, with visitors hanging paper, fabric, trinkets and ribbons. Some wrap colourful yarn and crochet round the trunk, echoing traditional May Day fertility celebrations in England, when dancers wrapped their ribbons round the maypole.

TECHNIQUE
Make Your Own Wishing Tree

1. Go to a favourite tree in your garden or yard. If you don't have a tree near you, you can gather some fallen branches from a park or woodland. If they're damp, let them dry out for a few days, then arrange them in a plant pot or other container. Secure them in position by packing the pot with twigs or stones, so they stand upright.
2. Write your wish on a biodegradable paper tag, or a small strip of natural fabric.

3. Think or speak aloud your wish, imagining it coming true.
4. Ask the tree for permission to approach, then gently tie your offering onto the tree.
5. Spend a few minutes reflecting on your wish, then give thanks to the tree.

You may not need to ask for anything at all, but simply want to leave an offering for your tree to thank it for the work it does. You might leave some fruit or flowers, a figurine, a stone you've painted or another hand-made gift.

TREE RITUAL
The Charm of Hope

In the early Irish tree-alphabet, the Ogham, each letter represents a particular tree. The letter Q in the alphabet is "quert", for apple tree. The letters STR are for "straif", the blackthorn tree. The apple (quert) relates to summer and light, while the blackthorn (straif) represents winter and darkness. Binding together a twig from each makes a totem representing the cycle of light throughout the year. As a personal charm, it brings hope and vision.

To represent apple and blackthorn, choose one light-coloured twig and one darker twig from any tree. Bind them together side by side using grass, reed, cord or thread. Dedicate your charm by asking it to work with you and repeating out loud three times your purpose or wish.

Then, thank the tree the twigs came from (if you found your twigs elsewhere on your walk, thank the tree nearest to you). Carry your new charm with you or place it on your altar.

You might designate your dark twig as representing the past, the ancestors and your unconscious self, and the light twig as the present, the practicalities of life and your conscious self. When you place the dark and light together, you see the whole picture before you.

Do this ritual on a new moon as this is the start of the moon's growth phase; it's a time of beginnings, new ideas and vision.

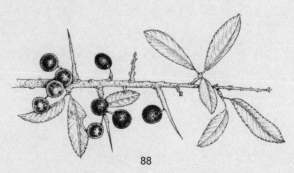

TREE RITUAL
Burying the Past

Bark, of course, is a protector, shielding the tree's living tissue from potential damage. However, as the bark is shed naturally from a tree as it ages, a charm of bark can also symbolize a wish for positive change.

Take a piece of fallen bark. Bring to mind a situation you need to let go of – an argument, a past relationship, a painful memory. Acknowledge the issue but try not to replay it. Don't allow anger to infect your ritual. It is not for the tree to take away anger, pain or irritation, but to carry your wish. As you hold the bark, tune in to your breathing, and very gradually slow down your breathing until you feel relaxed and calm (but breathe naturally; don't force it). Sense the freedom you will feel when the past is released and symbolically buried with the bark.

> "Don't allow anger to infect your ritual. It is not for the tree to take away anger, pain or irritation, but to carry your wish."

When you are ready, bury the bark beneath the tree it came from. Make a small hole in the earth near the roots, but without disturbing the root formation. The roots signify the past, so placing the bark here releases you from past issues. It affirms that you are ready for the positive changes ahead.

Perform this ritual during a waning moon. After the full moon, the visible moon wanes or decreases in size each night. This is a time for letting go – as the moon diminishes, so you gently release the past.

TREE RITUAL
The Luck and Protection Cross

This good-luck charm is traditionally made from two pieces of rowan wood (mountain ash), tied with red ribbon in the form of a cross. The rowan tree, also known as the wicken tree, witch tree and travellers' tree, has long been associated with psychic protection and warding off illness. Pieces of rowan were carried, or sewen into the lining of clothing, or placed around the home and outbuildings to break spells, protect against the evil eye, bring good luck and even guard against health complaints such as rheumatism. Such was the belief in the rowan's power of magic that even a small piece in your pocket would attract good fortune and keep away witches, fairies and other supernatural beings.

If on your walk you spy red rowan berries, take a closer look. (Please note that rowan berries are poisonous when eaten raw, though they are perfectly safe when cooked. NEVER eat any wild berries unless you can identify them and know they are perfectly safe.) You will see, without touching, the pentagram shape at the base – as if a star had been stamped on each one. The pentagram is an ancient symbol of protection, so this feature of the berry may have given the tree its old meaning of defence against enchantment.

As you may not necessarily see fallen rowan twigs on your walk, you can substitute any wood that gives you a feeling of strength and positivity. Choose small pieces of twig, and take a piece of long grass, vine, reed, cord or thread and bind the two pieces together in the shape of a cross. As you make a knot, declare that this charm will bring you all the luck and protection you need.

LEAF CHARMS

Like wood charms, leaf charms carry many of the same attributes of protection and luck. To our ancestors, because leaves appeared to float down from heaven, they carried a touch of celestial magic, which might just explain why they feature so often in tales of wishes granted. The children's game of catching falling autumn leaves is still enjoyed today (traditionally, every leaf caught gave one month of happiness). The lucky leaves of the ash tree were celebrated in the following English chant (the word "even" in the first line refers to the equal number of ovate leaves on each side of the stem):

> *"Even ash, I do thee pluck,*
> *Hoping thus to meet good luck.*
> *If no good luck I get from thee,*
> *I shall wish thee on the tree."*[3]

As leaves were messengers of luck and blessings, they also carried the healing power of the deities. In Cornwall, England, this charm was spoken to bramble leaves to soothe a scald:

> *"Three Ladies came from the East*
> *One with fire and two with frost.*
> *Out with thee, fire, and in with thee, frost."*[4]

The "enchanter" or healer, picked nine leaves from a bramble bush, dipped them in spring water and placed them over the scald, all the while reciting the charm three times to each leaf – a total of 27 times in all. The "Three Ladies" refers to the three aspects of the Celtic goddess Brigit: Brigit of Poetry, Brigit of Healing and Brigit of Smithcraft. The lady of fire must be Brigit of Smithcraft, and the ladies of frost – who will heal the scald – are the Brigits of Healing and Poetry. The bramble leaves bring the healing water to the wound, and the poetry is in the spoken charm. And so the enchanter invited the frost aspects of the goddess to work her magic through the leaves.

"The bay leaf is an 'intensifier' of energy."

LEAF RITUAL
Bay Laurel

Bay leaves for good fortune have many iterations. Their use dates back to Roman times when the laurel garland signified victory. You might write a wish on a bay leaf or think a wish into the leaf, then ritually burn it to symbolize the wish being delivered; or keep a bay leaf in your wallet or pocket for money luck. I think of the bay as an "intensifier" of energy – in that, positive intentions channelled into the leaf become more powerful.

One way to work with the energy of the bay is to dedicate a leaf to another person, someone you care about, who is in need. Take a dried bay leaf (you can dry your own or use one bought from a supermarket). Hold it and visualize the person you'd like to help. When you have their image fixed in your mind's eye, wrap them in pink light, representing love. Then write their name or initials on the underside of the leaf. Burn it safely to send up the wish, or carry it with you, or place it on your altar – whatever you feel guided to do.

TRADITIONAL TREE MEANINGS, QUALITIES AND USAGE

Below are the meanings, qualities and usage associated with a number of trees you may encounter on your walks. This is a selection from different cultural traditions, which is why there is such a range of interpretations. You will see that many trees take the meaning of protection (physical and/or psychic, a defence against bad luck and negative forces); trees bearing fruit with pips and seeds are fertility symbols; and evergreens are often trees of immortality, rebirth and renewal. In Celtic tradition, all wood ultimately means "learning" and "knowledge".

Acacia
Clairvoyance, spiritual secrets, immortality, rebirth

Alder
Protection, truth; tree of the fairies

Almond
Change, renewal, fertility, immortality, hope

Apple
Love, abundance, healing, knowledge, magic, prophecy, immortality

Ash
Protection, money, healing, love, luck, survival, stability, immortality

Aspen – *see* Poplar

Bamboo
Luck, flexibility, resilience, intuition, meditation

Bay Laurel (evergreen)
Immortality, success, victory, wisdom, money, psychic work, love, peace, cleansing

Beech
Writing, wishes

Birch
Protection, beginnings, fertility

Box (evergreen)
Perseverance, strength, immortality

Cedar (evergreen)
Healing, purity, money, moral strength, vitality

Cherry
Love, luck, prosperity; protection, beauty, immortality; carrying a small piece of cherry wood in your pocket was thought to protect against poison ivy

Chestnut
Anticipation, planning

Coconut (evergreen)
Protection, chastity

Cypress (evergreen)
Immortality, rebirth, the underworld, purity

Elder
Change, healing, sleep, protection

Elm
Sanctuary, love, willpower, intuition, the underworld; tree of the fairies

Eucalyptus (evergreen)
Healing, cleansing, energy, healing the past

Fig
Abundance, religious knowledge, fertility, love divination (casting the leaves)

Fir (evergreen)
Immortality, truth, friendship, loyalty, renewal, hope, resilience

Hawthorn
Luck, fertility, chastity, happiness, travel protection, psychic protection, death and birth; portal to fairyland

Hazel

Wisdom, luck, fertility, wishes, magic, protection while travelling, divination (dowsing with a hazel rod)

Holly (evergreen)

Protection, peace, hope, luck, success, balance

Ivy (evergreen)

Cycles of life, desire, rebirth

Juniper/Eastern Red Cedar (evergreen)

Love, protection, purification

Larch

Protection, immortality

Lemon

Cleansing, healing, joy, energy

Lilac

Clairvoyance, protection, beauty

Lime or linden

Protection, healing, love, immortality, luck, sleep

Magnolia (evergreen)

Loyalty, wisdom, calmness

Mahogany (evergreen)
Protection, strength

Maple
Love, longevity, money, optimism

Mimosa
Power, transformation, love, prophetic dreams

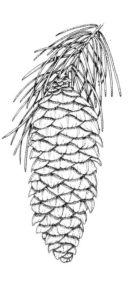

Mulberry
Strength, protection, support

Myrtle
Love, fertility, youth, peace

Oak
Wisdom, healing, longevity, luck, fertility, money, strength, success, divination (using Ogham, the old Irish tree alphabet, inscribed wood was cast to divine the future)

Olive (evergreen)
Abundance, healing, success, reward, peace, protection, fertility, lust

Orange (evergreen)
Love, fertility, luck, money, happiness, divination (by counting the number of pips inside – even number means "yes", odd number means "no")

Date Palm (evergreen)
Fertility, honesty, prosperity

Pear
Sensuality, love, lust

Peach
Immortality, fertility, divination (in China, the wood was used to make brushes for writing prophetic symbols)

Pecan
Money, prosperity, security, abundance

Pine (evergreen)
Immortality, longevity, healing, fertility, cleansing, clarity, good fortune

Plantain
Healing, protection, strength, fertility, pregnancy

Plum
Renewal, purity, healing, immortality

Poplar (Aspen)
The past, memories, the underworld, money, communication

Redwood (Sequoia)
Protection, healing, knowledge, abundance

Rowan
Psychic protection, discernment, luck, travel protection, divination (aids spiritual connection when dried leaves are crumbled and burned like incense)

Sycamore
Immortality, wisdom

Vine (evergreen)
Immortality, knowledge, abundance

Walnut
Prophecy, health, focus, wishes

Willow
Grief, healing, comfort, wishes, dreaming, immortality, divination (used for water divining, known as "willow witching")

Yew (evergreen)
Defence, death, immortality, the afterlife, rebirth

4

Fruit, Nuts and Seeds

Fertility and Divination

Seeds, fruits, nuts and cones have long been associated with fertility, longevity and renewal. The British tradition of throwing confetti at weddings comes from the casting of wheat grains over a married couple to ensure their fertility in the coming years. In Nordic mythology, the apple tree symbolizes immortality, related in the tale of the goddess Idunn ("ever-young") who stored magic apples in a box made of ash wood; she gave them to all the other gods and goddesses to ensure their enduring youth and fertility. Hazel leaves and nuts were found in the graves of early Celtic peoples, particularly in Norfolk, England[15], to accompany the deceased to the other world, where they rested before being reincarnated – so beginning a new cycle of life.

According to Walter Scott's *Minstrelsy of the Scottish Border*, fern seeds, known to be "under the special protection of the Queen of Faerie", made a person invisible at will and bestowed power and wealth in the form of hidden gold. They were famously difficult to gather, because it was forbidden to touch the plant – only fallen seeds could be collected between 11pm and midnight on Midsummer Eve when the plant flowered and instantly produced its seed. Adding to the precarious nature of the quest, spirits might attack you while you patiently waited for the tiny harvest. After all, they did not want power falling into the wrong hands. The tale is a metaphor for seeds as gold: a symbol of life, sunshine and abundance.

DIVINATION RITUALS

Seeds and fruits have been popular as love charms and for love divination down the centuries and across many cultures. Many fruit trees, such as the pear, peach, apple and cherry, are associated with love, sexuality, fertility and sensuality. A whole fruit containing a host of seeds or pips, such as the pomegranate or the gourd, signified great fertility for generations to come. Nuts and other fruits take a similar meaning, often with the addition of abundance, which relates to when the growth cycle is complete and the nuts and fruits are ready for harvesting. Seeds represent the beginning of a new cycle, while nuts and fruits are the ripened outcome. There are a multitude of superstitions and rituals involving fruit, nuts and other seeds, from divining with pips to consult the gods, to making a love charm that sends out a wish for romance. In the Ozarks, young women once wore a carved peach stone or a cherry stone with an unknown "pinkish, soap-like material inside."[16] The charm was worn as a pendant or attached to a garter to attract love.

In divination, pips, fruit stones, nuts, seeds and small fruits lend themselves to prophesy, not only because of their associations with love, but because they come in multiples. Ask a question, count the number of pips or seeds in your piece of fruit – an apple or orange, for example – and you have an answer: an even number meant "yes"; an odd number meant "no". In some children's games, rhymes accompanied the counting, such as "loves me, loves me not", spoken while picking out pips from an apple core or counting cherry stones, or chanting "Tinker, tailor, soldier, sailor, rich man, poor man, beggarman, thief (or chief)", if you wanted to find out your future career or what kind of man you were destined to marry.

On one magical night of the year – such as Midsummer Eve, Hallowe'en (Samhain) or Christmas Eve, young European women took to the churchyard at midnight; throwing hempseed over their left shoulder, they chanted:

"Hempseed I sow, Hempseed, grow.
He that is to marry me
Come after me and mow."[7]

If they saw a ghost of a man when they turned around, they would get married that year. The apparition was the future husband, mowing behind them, scythe in hand.

To meet a future husband in the flesh, a woman would need to practise "peascod wooing" – find a pea pod with nine peas inside (the unripe pea being the plant's seed) and hang it over a doorway with white thread. She would marry the next eligible man who came through the door. Likewise, women took sweet chestnuts, naming each one after a potential suitor. They put the nuts to roast on the fire, singing this charm:

"Maidens, name your chestnuts true
The first to burst belongs to you!"[8]

At the other end of the spectrum is the association with death as part of the natural cycle. One strange piece of lore from Northamptonshire in England, cited in *The Folk-lore Record* (1879), relates how children sang the following words around a cherry tree:

"Cuckoo, cherry tree
How many years am I to live
One, two, three."

The idea was that the cuckoo would cry once for every year the child had to live, or in other versions, each child shook the tree and counted the number of fallen cherries. The cuckoo here represents the spirit of the tree (the Baltic goddess Laima, for example, took the form of a cuckoo in a lime tree). It seems the cherry-tree children were calling to the old deities for a prediction, which they hopefully did not take too seriously. There are a number of variations of the rhyme, which was also popular in France and Germany.

Fruits, Nuts and Seeds Charm Examples

Seeds, sycamore and ash seeds (keys), nutshells, nuts, pips, fruits, berries, pine cones.

SEED RITUAL
Seeds of Intention

Working with seeds as symbols of creative power can help you seed ideas and grow a project.

When you're out walking, gather seed heads. On flowering plants they may look faded and dry, or appear as fluffy, geometric balls, as with the allium and dandelion. You might find the large, rounded seed pods of wild poppies, or rub the ears of dry grasses to harvest their seeds as you stroll.

When you have gathered your seeds, find a place in nature to rest. Cup the seeds in both hands to make a "container" for your wish. Then, blow your wish through your thumbs to the seeds. Do this three times.

At home, plant the seeds in the earth and nurture them to represent your manifesting wish, or place them in a glass jar with a feather you have found on one of your walks. The feather takes your wish up to the universe. Hold the jar in both hands, give thanks for the seeds and feather, and place it on your altar, desk or wherever it's easy to see, so you do not lose sight of the jar or your desire.

You can also add your seeds to your herb pouch (see pages 118–119).

SEED RITUAL
Dandelion Wishes

The dandelion is linked with spontaneity and wishes, probably due to its magical transformation from ragged flower to puff-ball. Its seeds, poised to fly, evoke wishes on the wind. You can blow on a puff-ball to transmit a wish or use it for divination.

Bring your wish to mind, then blow hard on the puff-ball. If all the seeds fly off at once, you will get your wish almost at once. If a few seeds remain, your wish is granted but will take some time to manifest. If most of the seeds are left, you may not get your wish at all.

This ritual was used in love divination to find out if the person you wanted would love you in return.

TRADITIONAL NUT AND SEED MEANINGS, QUALITIES AND USAGE

Below are the meanings, qualities and usage associated with some of the nuts and seeds you may see on your walks. The meanings are less varied than those given for tree meanings; from China and ancient Greece to Italy and Egypt, seeds and nuts were commonly associated with money and fertility, and in some instances, divination (counting seeds).

Almond
Money, prosperity, wisdom

Acorn
Fertility, truth, protection (an acorn on a windowsill protected the home from lightning)

Chestnut
Fertility, foresight (it is an edible food in winter)

Hazelnut
Knowledge, inspiration, wealth, fertility, marriage

Pine cone
Fertility, renewal

Walnut
Intellect, prophecy, fertility, love, marriage

Ash seed
Attention, to be visible

Dandelion seed
Fertility, divination

Poppy seed
Prosperity, happiness

Sunflower seed
Fertility, wishes

Sycamore seed
Security, oneness

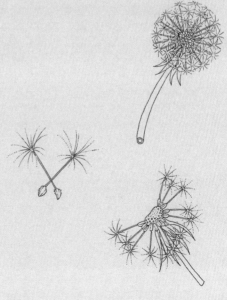

5

Herbs

Healing and Magic

Across many cultures, the village cunning folk – the original herbalists and wise ones – were expert foragers and healers. A healing charm was a herbal cure, accompanied often by a spoken charm muttered while making the potion and tending the patient. We may have lost much of their knowledge, but we can follow in their footsteps to build relationships with plants and create our own song charms for protection, cleansing, luck and positivity.

"Consider that every plant you encounter has a purpose, and generate a feeling of appreciation for what it provides."

FINDING YOUR HERBS

Small or straggling, some herbs may disappear under our gaze because we unconsciously seek what is unusual or classically beautiful. They might appear by a road or a path as we breeze past, looking for something more visually arresting. Yet, when you open your senses on a walk (see pages 32–33), you will find yourself more sensitive to all the life around you. You can stop as often as you like to take in the smallest herb and discover more about it. Consider that every plant you encounter has a purpose, and generate a feeling of appreciation for what it provides. You do not need to know what healing properties these plants have (that is a book in itself); when you give gratitude to plants for their existence, you make your walk all the more magical. It's a reciprocal arrangement.

You may find you rediscover plants that you have taken for granted because they are all too common where you live. I walked past the little mats of moss on oak trunks for months before I stopped to look closely. This plant felt very protective – a green coat for the tree. Druids believed moss had the power to ward off accidents; and in Irish folk medicine, a moss spell was used to bring down inflammation; Margaret Baker's *Discovering the Folklore of Plants* tells us that nine handfuls of mountain moss were picked, then dried to a powder: "Nine pinches of this with nine pinches of ashes from the hearth (a magical place) were mixed in whey and taken every Tuesday and Thursday." Even turf had its magical uses. To protect against witchcraft and ill-wishes, you'd take a piece of turf and wear it under your hat – the double magic of earth and grass setting up a kind of psychic shield. Even the humblest herb has a hidden tradition, and often a magical purpose.

CONNECTING WITH THE PLANT

When you're choosing a herb charm, remember the *genius loci* – the spirit of place (see pages 51–52) – and ask the plant permission to take a little sample. (As ever, it's advisable to touch only herbs you know are safe.) Spend a few minutes together, holding your find and feeling the plant's vibration. You may see its aura (see pages 42–45) and sense how it wants to work with you.

You can work with a single herb charm or use a number of herbs together to make a composite charm.

Herb Charm Examples

Whole herb, sprig, leaf, flower, stem.

HERB ACTIVATION

To activate your herb, dedicate it to your purpose and/or tie it with thread or vine, with the knot sealing your intention (see pages 46–47).

In charm-work, there's always an activator – an action that directs your wish and makes the charm operate for you. Even in the simplest practices, there is a physical action, from hammering a coin into a wishing tree or hanging a tie on a branch to stirring a potion three times in a certain direction. These actions make the intention real and visible. With herb charms, there are many examples of special charms or incantations that are spoken or sung over the plant: the words create the intended reality, the magic that is to come.

"In charm-work, there's always an activator – an action that directs your wish. These actions make the intention real and visible."

The ability to create magic with words is embedded into every culture, and one fine description of this is related by the scholar William Ralston, who explains how in Slavic tradition the magic of the spoken word was likened to a key turning two locks. The locks are the teeth and tips, which are undone by the tongue. Then, "out shoots the word ... and it is capable of flying straight to, and acting directly upon, the object at which it is aimed by its utterer."[19] Powerful words indeed.

With all this in mind, you might like to create a ritual song for each plant, naming it and its properties. One approach is to follow the Anglo-Saxon nine-herb charm:

"Remember, Chamomile, what you made known,
What you accomplished at Aloford,
That never a man should lose his life from infection,
After Chamomile was prepared for his food."

The charmer speaks directly to the plants and recalls the herb's past heroic deeds, talking to it like an old friend. If you were using lavender, for example, you might chant:

"Lavender, you are known for serenity
Grant my wish for peace and harmony
So mote it be."

Including rhyme gives the lines rhythm and energy. A ritual phrase from Wiccan and Pagan tradition ends the above charm. "So mote it be" ("mote" meaning "must") is used here, but you can use "Amen", "Thank you", or another phrase you like instead.

TECHNIQUE
Making a Herb Pouch

Herb pouches, also known as witch sachets or charm bags, are used to carry herb medicine for mind, body and spirit. It's a time-honoured way to benefit from the collective energy of herbs and other charms you find. You'll need a small tie-string pouch made of lightweight fabric, such as cotton, muslin or organza, and a length of cord or ribbon if you want to wear your pouch around your neck.

Keeping a herb pouch close to you throughout the day – in your bag or pocket, or worn as a pendant – acts as a constant reminder of your positive intentions and wishes.

Choose three herbs, or multiples of three. The number three represents a creative cycle and the dynamic energy of fire (see also Chapter 11).

You can see the herb meanings on pages 126–131 for guidance, or choose your preferred (non-toxic) herbs. Bring in other charms alongside the herbs – for example, small pieces of twig or bark, nuts, seeds and shells. Again, keep to three and its multiples when you're finalizing your selection. Here are some examples:

For strength: Thistle flower, oak leaf, columbine
For calm: Lavender, moss, mint
For protection: Thyme, rowan wood, shell
For luck and success: Clover, daisy, fern
For love: Apple leaf, rose petal, ivy

Always sense what the plant means to you and go with your intuition. You might discover that the combination, say, of a flower petal, a sycamore seed and a feather feels like the perfect choice.

Decide if you'd like to keep your herbs whole or to tear them up. When you bruise or tear the leaves you release the aroma, which helps fix the positive memory of your walk. If you smell your herbs when you're away from nature, the aroma can act as a memory-trigger, taking you back to the experience of your charm walk. This happens because the olfactory bulb in the forebrain connects to the amygdala and hippocampus, which handle emotion and memory.

Activate each herb (see pages 115–117) and when your pouch is ready, recite the dedication once more, then pull the drawstring and knot in a bow to seal in your dedication. Carry the pouch with you in your bag or pocket, or attach a cord and wear it round your neck. Wear or carry it for as long as you need to. When you sense it has done its work, return the herb and other finds to nature, and offer a moment of gratitude.

If you have any crystals, you can add them to your herb pouch. Here are some examples:

For strength: Carnelian, turquoise, jasper
For calm: Amethyst, moonstone, selenite
For protection: Tiger's eye, amber, obsidian
For luck and success: Citrine, jade, sunstone
For love: Rose quartz, rhodonite, aventurine

CHARM BOTTLES AND
SHADOWBOXES

Charm bottles and shadowbox lockets, which can both be obtained online or from specialist stores, are designed to be worn as pendants.

A charm bottle is a small vial made of glass with a stopper, usually in the shape of a cylinder or teardrop.

A shadowbox locket is a tiny picture frame with a door, deep enough to display charms in miniature.

This is where you can explore the tiny detail of your herbs, choosing anything from dandelion seeds to a mint bud or a flake of bark.

HERBS FOR DREAMING

Certain herbs are said to bring on certain types of dream when placed under the pillow at night. These herbs, whether known from spiritual practices in ancient Greece and Rome or from European folklore, seem to have two principal purposes: to promote dreams of a future partner or to ward off bad dreams. What's interesting here is that the herbs appear to fall into two groups – ruled either by Venus and Mercury, or the sun (the ruling planets idea comes from 17th-century English doctor and astrologer Nicholas Culpeper in *Complete Herbal*).

Mercury is the planet of communication and Venus is the planet of love, so either planet works for getting a message about love. Marjoram, ruled by Mercury, and mugwort and yarrow, ruled by Venus, were believed to bring dreams of future lovers.

The sun, planet of optimism and happiness, rules over St John's Wort, chamomile and rosemary – a sprig of one of these herbs would ward off bad dreams.

If you're interested in astrology and herbs, see which planets govern the herbs found local to you – they might just make the perfect dream herbs to place in a pouch under your pillow.

TECHNIQUE
Pressing Herbs and Flowers

When our time in nature is rare, pressed plants offer a reminder that the wild world is still there. And because you choose the plants, the pressed herbs and flowers may tell a more intimate story of your walk than any photograph.

1. Take a piece of printer paper and on one half arrange your herbs and flowers, leaving space between each object.
2. Fold over the other half of the paper, forming an open envelope, and place it inside a heavy book.
3. Stack more heavy books or other weights on top and leave to dry for two to three weeks. Note that the herbs and flowers will wrinkle the book's pages as they dry out; if you don't want this to happen, place the folded paper on top of the book with an extra sheet of paper and cardboard under and above it to protect the book cover.
4. When dry, remove each herb or flower using tweezers, as they can be fragile.
5. You can dry small specimens and place them in your shadowbox (see page 120), or use larger pieces to make a seasonal picture for your altar.

TECHNIQUE
Drying Whole Herbs

First, find the perfect place for herb-drying; you'll need a well-aerated spot away from direct sunlight.

1. Take a single stem or make small bundles of herbs according to type and tie together at the stem.
2. Knot a length of string round the binding and wrap the bundle loosely with a paper bag or muslin if you're worried about mess – as the herbs or flowers dry, they will shed seeds and smaller petals.
3. Hang the stem or bundle upside down, leaves downward, from a hook or a nail in a wall or a ceiling, so the herbs can move freely and air can reach them on all sides.

You'll need to leave them to dry for a week or so, depending on the temperature of the room and its airiness.

To transform your drying herbs into a house charm, dedicate the bundle to work for you (see pages 46–47) and seal your intention by focusing your thoughts on it as you make knots in the string (for more on knots, see Chapter 6).

HERB RITUAL
Cleansing with a
Herb Smudge Stick

Used originally by indigenous peoples, smudge sticks are bound bundles of cleansing herbs that are burned during spiritual ceremonies. The practice is known as "smudging", which purifies energy. Many people today smudge to clear out unwanted or negative energy in a space. Sage is the prime ingredient in smudge sticks, to which other herbs can be added – traditional choices are lavender, rosemary, mugwort, rose petals, sweetgrass, thyme, pine and cedar. You can also choose mint, bay laurel, fern and eucalyptus. If you don't have any sage, improvise – it's fine to work with just pine or lavender or, say, mint or bay; all these herbs have natural cleansing properties. You can use dried herbs from stores or online suppliers, too.

> "'Smudging' purifies energy. Many people smudge to clear out unwanted or negative energy in a space."

Gather your herbs into a small bunch and cut it to a length of around 10–15cm (4–6in). If you're adding in petals or leaves, intersperse them with the herb stalks. Tie your herbs together at the base with strong grass or cord. Wrap them with the cord or string from the base to the tip, then down again from the tip to the base so you make a criss-cross pattern. Secure with a knot at the base. If you're using fresh plants, hang them up to dry for around a week (depending on your climate). If you're using dried plants, you can use your smudge stick straight away.

Light the stick and hold it over a small, heat-proof bowl to catch the ash as you walk around the space. Use your hand or a large feather to waft the smoke upward, downward and into corners, as the smoke smudges, or purifies, any residual energy in the room. Continue until the room's atmosphere feels lighter.

To finish, turn to the four compass points – first the north, then the south, then the east and finally the west. Pause for a moment each time, feeling thankful that your space is now cleansed. Finish by saying:

"North, south, east and west
My home is cleansed and now is blessed
So mote it be."

125

TRADITIONAL PLANT AND HERB MEANINGS, QUALITIES AND USAGE

Below are the meanings, qualities and usage associated with a number of plants and herbs you may encounter on your walks. This selection hails from different cultural traditions, which is why there can be such a range of interpretations.

Barley
Love, healing, protection

Basil
Money, mental focus, clarity

Bay leaf
Immortality, success, victory, wisdom, money, psychic work, love, peace, cleansing

Blackberry
Healing, money, protection

Bluebell
Luck, truth

Borage
Courage, happiness

Bracken
Healing, prophetic dreams

Broom
Purification, protection

Burdock
Healing, fertility, money

Buttercup
Joy, beginnings

Chamomile
Money, sleep, love, purification

Chickweed
Fertility, love

Clover
Protection, discretion, money, love, luck, success
   Four-leaved clover: seeing fairies; being granted a wish by fairies

Columbine
Courage, love

Corn
Protection, luck

Cornflower
Healing, psychic work

Cowslip
Healing, finding treasure

Daisy
Luck, innocence

Dandelion
Travel, wishes, divination, manifesting (by making a wish on a puff-ball, then blowing on it)

Dill
Love, protection

Dock *see* Burdock

Elderflower
Love, happy relationships

Fern
Luck, money, protection

Gorse
Protection, money

Grass
Psychic powers, protection

Heather
Luck, protection
White heather: happiness, safe journeys

Honesty (moonwort)
Psychic protection, shape-shifting, recovering lost items

Honeysuckle
House protection, romantic luck

Hyssop
Cleansing, protection

Ivy
Protection, perseverance, healing, fidelity, fertility, mysticism

Knotweed
Health, growth, commitment

Lavender
Love, protection, serenity, harmony, sleep, clairvoyance (by burning the dry herb or essential oil to aid "sight")

Marjoram
Love, happiness, purification

Mint
Clarity, money, love, luck, healing, travel, protection

Mistletoe
Prophecy (meaning), strength, healing, rebirth, immortality, love, fertility, protection

Moss
Luck, money, prevents accidents

Mugwort
Protection, energy, psychic work, wisdom

Nettle
Courage, protection, healing, fertility, lust

Poppy
Fertility, love, sleep, money, luck, invisibility

Reed
Manifesting (meaning), cleansing, protection, wealth, truth, music

Rosemary
Memory, physical and psychic protection

Rose
Love, growth, renewal

Rye
Love, fidelity

Sage
Wisdom, wishes, longevity, protection

St John's Wort
Happiness, optimism, psychic connection and protection

Sunflower
Fame, fertility, longevity

Sweetgrass
Purification, calling in spirits

Thistle
Defence, strength

Thyme
Protection from psychic attack, purification, courage

Vervain
Money, love, protection

Wheat
Fertility, money

Yarrow
Protection, love, strengthening relationships, psychic protection

6

Grasses and Vines

Knot Magic and Protection

Whenever you use a knot to make a charm, you are using knot magic. A knot has power – it binds in your wish and is a personal signature for your charm. "Tie a knot in your handkerchief, and you'll remember", the saying goes – an echo of the knot as a symbol of intention.

While knots are a part of composite charms (one that has two or more items tied together), knot charms can also stand alone – a string with knots tied in it is simply a knot charm. You can make one with cord, raffia, wool or thread or better still, use "nature's string" – grasses and vines.

In Celtic tradition, knot charms were popular at critical stages or events in life: at birth, during illness, as protection from illness, in love and in fear of death. A person would tie the knotted thread or wool round their body for protection – the idea was that the knots contained the problem and kept the wearer from harm. Then, when the danger had passed, the knots were loosened and good luck was sure to flow.

In one folk remedy from central Asia, to cure a fever, a healer or "enchanter" spun a thread from camel hair and tied it in seven knots.[20] The enchanter blew on each knot after he tied it, uttering a charm as he worked. The patient wore the knot charm as a bracelet, and each day the healer untied one knot and blew upon it. On the seventh day, when all the knots were undone, the bracelet was cast into the river. The water took away the charm and the last of the fever.

This unknotting spell was evident in sea lore, too. In the 19th century, folklorist Walter Gregor told of a sailor from Portessie, Scotland, who related how the crew had a length of twine with three knots in it. He says:

"One knot was to be loosed when the sail was hoisted. The second was to be loosed after a time to freshen the wind. All went well for a time, but after a little it fell 'breath-calm.' The third knot was loosed, but hardly was this done when a storm burst upon us, and we hardly escaped with [our] life ..."[21]

In love magic, knots and circles represent love and marriage, hence the saying "getting hitched" or "tying the knot". This comes from the Celtic tradition of handfasting, when a couple's joined hands were tied with cord, cloth, ribbon or braid to signify binding their lives together.

While knot charms were generally made with cord, twine, wool, thread or ribbon, you can work with whatever you discover on your walks. When choosing plant material for knotting, avoid anything too dry and brittle or your loops will break.

KNOT RITUAL
A Knotty Problem

If a problem is playing on your mind, tie it up in a knot before it overshadows your walk. Fetch a stalk of grass or other plant material (see above), and tie one knot in it. Send all your thoughts and emotions about

EXAMPLES OF MATERIAL FOR KNOTS

Long wild grasses; cereal crops (rye, corn, barley); sea grass; herb stems; ivy, beanstalks and other vines; some types of seaweed.

Test the strength of your chosen "string" before working with it. The most flexible are climbing plant stems, such as vines and beanstalks, which naturally knot together.

this situation into the knot as you tie it. This issue is now locked up, and you won't need to think about it again until your walk is over, as the knot protects you from unwanted worry.

If you have more than one issue, take another stalk and tie a knot in it to represent that problem, and repeat – but stick to a maximum of three knotted blades or stalks. Otherwise, you get focussed on counting problems – when you would rather be looking at trees or finding feathers.

Carry your knotted stalk or stalks with you but keep them out of sight. Holding them may only remind you of what you don't need to think about just now.

When your walk is at an end, take out your stalks, untie the knots and cast into running water (if you can't do this, give the stalks to the wind). Doing so releases the problem(s) and gets fresh energy flowing. Before you leave, give thanks to nature.

In the next few hours, you should have a new perspective on your situation.

KNOT RITUAL
A Braid for Love to Flourish

This ritual is perfect if you want your relationship to grow stronger. When you make this charm in nature, find a strong, healthy tree and sit by it, as you will need to bury your charm by its roots when you have finished.

A simple grass braid has three plaited strands. The number three signifies you, your partner and your relationship. Plaiting the strands into a braid binds you together. To begin, find your braiding material, and sit comfortably by your chosen tree. Take three stems and knot them together at the top. Then make a braid, just as you would plait hair. Your knotted braid needs to be several inches long, so you can tie it into the shape of a ring by knotting both ends together (if this is difficult, leave it flat and finish it by knotting at each end).

While you make the braid, think about all the positives in your relationship and how you would like to see it develop. You can say the following words, or compose your own spoken charm:

"Let our love be true,
One for me, two for you
Three for lasting harmony.
So mote it be."

Say this three times. When you are ready, take your knot charm and bury it by the roots of your tree. Give thanks to the tree before you go. As the tree continues to flourish, so will your relationship.

DECORATING YOUR LOVE BRAID

You can further empower your love braid by adding in some small finds, such as feathers, flowers or herb sprigs. Making your charm decorative affirms your wish for a relationship that grows beautifully.

KNOT RITUAL
The Aspen Star for Inspiration and Joy

You can make this little star charm to carry with you in your bag or pocket.

Take three twigs and two lengths of vine. First, tie the first two twigs into an "X" shape by binding the vine round them. Work carefully and pull your first knot gently so the vine doesn't break. Then add your third twig to make a six-pronged star, and bind and knot it again with another piece of vine. Try to make the tightest knots you can without breaking the vine, because as the vine dries out, it will shrink – and the knots can become too loose to hold the twigs in place. Alternatively, use cord, thread, string or raffia instead, so you can bind the twigs more tightly together.

If you don't have aspen trees near you, use any wood you feel drawn to. Dedicate your wood charm by chanting:

"Star charm I dedicate thee
To inspiration, joy and beauty
So mote it be."

THE POWER OF IVY

Back in the late 19th and early 20th centuries, the humble ivy was worn as a charm of protection. An ivy charm necklace is part of the collection of English naturalist and folklorist William James Clarke (1871–1945). The necklace has threaded tubular beads, and is a rare surviving example of a botanical charm.

TECHNIQUE
Vine Beads for Protection

You can make vine beads for your herb pouch or altar, or thread them into a bracelet. Find a fresh vine with a wide stem and choose a straightish section. (Please note that dried vine will not work, as it's too tough to pierce.) As the vine dries, it shrinks to around two-thirds of its original thickness, so bear this in mind when selecting your vine.

1. Take your length of vine and chop it into equal-length sections about the length of your thumb nail.
2. Leave it to dry for up to three days, because the vine is too tough to pierce when fresh.
3. Take a needle or a skewer and push it through the centre of each length from end to end to make a bead, then thread a needle with wool or cotton thread, and string the beads together, securing them with a knot.

Before you use your beads, ask yourself what you need protection from. When you are clear about the help you need, dedicate your beads to your purpose (see pages 46–47). The beads can last many months. If you wear them as a bracelet they may only last up to five days due to wear and tear, but, after that, you can place the bracelet as a charm on your altar.

TECHNIQUE
Making a Vine Bangle

A vine bangle is simple to make, as all you need is a piece of naturally curved vine.

1. Cut it to the length of your hand, and gently bend it into a circle.
2. Twist the ends over each other and leave for a minute or two – if the twists don't unravel, leave the bracelet to dry for a day or so.
3. If it begins to come undone, twist it again or bind it with a little thread to secure it.

The bangle can last for up to five days, if worn. In a herb pouch or as an altar charm, it will last for many months.

7

Stones

Wisdom-keepers

With every stone, you hold a piece of history. A little rock may have taken thousands or even millions of years to come to you, and its shape, colour and texture tells its incredible story.

"Stone physically and metaphorically represents ancient wisdom, transformation, strength and healing."

Find a stone now and look at it closely. It may be sedimentary, such as sandstone or chalk (rocks formed from pieces of other rocks or from compressed fossils), which changes shape through erosion. It may be igneous ("of fire"), formed from cooled lava, like basalt or granite. Or it may be metamorphic, like marble or slate, which is created when rock is subjected to intense heat and pressure. You could be looking at a meteorite, which makes a 30-million-mile journey through space to Earth. (Because they come down from the sky, meteorites were once known as "talking stones", or messengers of the gods.) Your stone could have a fossil or chips of embedded shell or other minerals, telling a tale of its evolution. Equally, you might have a plain piece of limestone or compressed coal left over from local mining or quarrying that has only travelled a short distance to find you, but holds the story of the people who worked those mines – ancestors, even. Whatever you have in your palm is a record of events that have occurred here on Earth and in space.

Perhaps for these reasons, stone physically and metaphorically represents ancient wisdom, transformation, strength and healing. Because a stone seems to live eternally, it gains a connection with the divine. Stones were cast to consult the old gods, a technique reputedly invented in Europe by three nymphs at the Greek oracle's site of Delphi; they used little stones to tell fortunes. These stones were called *mantic*, meaning "prophecy".

Stones continue to intrigue and inspire us, and it feels so natural to pick them up. Holding a stone brings its wisdom all the closer to us.

TRANSFORMATION STONES

In folklore and fairy tales, a stone acts as a transformer, a magic ingredient. Remember the old European tale of stone soup? When villages won't give hungry travellers any food, the travellers fill a cooking pot with water from the stream, set it on a fire and drop a stone in the water. When curious villagers pass by, the travellers say they are making stone soup, which tastes delicious – just a few more ingredients are needed. Soon enough, the villagers contribute carrots, seasoning and other vegetables, and the soup is shared by all. In another European story, the fairy tale of *The Invisible Prince*, a fairy gives a young prince a stone that makes him invisible whenever he puts it in his mouth. He uses the fairy's gift to find a kidnapped princess and pleads with the fairy for another stone to make the princess invisible too, so they can escape together.

In both these tales, the stone comes to symbolize ingenuity – and it magnifies the wish of the person who possesses it. Even birds can have magic stones, as in the German tale of the tiny siskin, a type of finch. The siskin had a magic stone in its nest that made the bird invisible during the breeding season. Another telling of the tale substitutes the stone with magic eggs. The stone or eggs are the catalysts, the means by which we can shift from one state of being to another.

ENCHANTMENT AND HEALING STONES

In the folklore of many cultures, stones have long been a symbol of enchantment, healing and protection. A toadstone, a magic stone supposed to be found in the head of the toad, was believed to be a charm for healing and protection. It was reputed to cure bites and stings at a touch, protect pregnant women from demons, and could change colour to warn the bearer when poison was afoot.

This might sound like a fairy tale, but the toadstone was real. It was likely formed inside the toad from the teeth of an extinct fish. Toadstones date back to medieval times when the small, button-like "stones" were set into rings and amulets. One may have made its way into Walter Scott's possession; in his collection of ballads, *Minstrelsy of the Scottish Border*, Scott reveals that "various monstrous charms" existed to banish a demon that had taken over a child. In a footnote, he says,

"The editor is possessed of a small relique, termed by tradition a toadstone, the influence of which was supposed to preserve pregnant women from the power of daemons, and other dangers incidental to their situation. It has been carefully preserved for generations, was often pledged for considerable sums of money ..."[22]

Slavic folklore has the "fiery stone" known as Alatuir, which was revered for its healing properties. It was said that either a mythical deity or a maiden who stitched up bleeding wounds sat on the stone. Norse mythology has the Skofnung stone, which healed wounds made by the sword of the same name. Some healing stones were known as charm stones, which were dipped in water or boiled in other liquid such as milk, with the fluid then applied to heal sickness.

STONE RITUAL
Stones for Divination and Charms

Stones reveal absolutes, what is "set in stone". This ritual comes originally from the Hebrew Bible, which mentions two sacred stones, named as Urim and Thummin, used by the high priest to reveal the will of God (the absolute truth). Author Paulo Coelho in his novel *The Alchemist* interprets Urim and Thummin as "yes" and "no" divination stones.

To begin, find a black or dark-coloured stone and a light or white stone. Give a "yes" or "no" meaning to each (white does not have to be "yes" – it could be your "no"). Then find a "marker" object, such as a larger stone, a leaf, a twig or a shell. Hold the stones in your cupped palms over the marker and connect with the stones' vibration through the chakra visualization (see pages 43–44). Think about the question you'll ask. When you are ready, close your eyes, speak your question out loud, and release the stones. The stone that lands closest to the marker object is the answer.

Two-Stone Charm

You can make a charm from your two stones. Meanings of Urim and Thummim include "revelation and truth" or "teaching and truth". So you might ask this charm to bring clarity, new information and learning, for example. Dedicate your stones to your purpose, then bind the two stones together using cord or grass. Add a knot to secure the charm to seal your intention.

STONE RITUAL
A Quick Way to Ground and Balance

This practice is an instant way to get out of over-thinking. If stressful thoughts intrude while you're out walking, try this.

Pick up two stones of similar weight and size. Tune in to each stone's vibration (you might also sense their history). If possible, sit down in a sheltered, comfortable spot. Hold one stone in each palm, as if weighing it, with your palms loosely cupped. Take your attention to your breathing, and visualize that you are mixing your breath with the energy emitting from the stones. Feel the sense of balance this brings, and stay with this feeling for as long as you need to.

When you are finished, give gratitude and slowly walk on.

STONE RITUAL
Lucky Stones

White stones are seen as lucky and, in folklore, all kinds of white stones were good-luck charms. In 1914, a teacher in Wales observed how a boy picked up a white stone from the road, spat on it and threw it over his head. The boy said:

"Lucky, lucky stone
Bring me luck, when I go home."[23]

Afterwards, to keep the luck, he had to make sure he didn't look back when walking round a corner.

Pick up a small, white stone on your walks, and carry it with you for good fortune – or, if you're inclined, follow the boy's old ritual.

STONE RITUAL
Travel Charms

A stone washed in seawater is said to be a travel charm, guiding you wherever you need to go. Traditionally, the stone you choose should be fish-shaped, but I would interpret this as being the shape of a fish's body – like an almond or a rough oval.

Take the charm to the sea and dip it in the water. If it's too far to walk to the water or it is not safe to do so, find a rock pool or rivulet in the sand and dip it there. Hold your charm and see where it takes you.

If you can't get to the sea often, choose a fish-shaped stone from one of your walks and keep it so you can do this ritual the next time you visit the sea.

STONE RITUAL
Making a Meandering Path of Life

The pathway in this ritual symbolizes journeying and our path in life. It's a helpful symbol to work with if you are struggling to accept change and need to trust that it is safe to go with the flow.

> "The joy of this practice comes through the creative journey rather than the goal of completion."

In this ritual you create an S-shape to represent your life path. You make the S-shape outdoors with stones and any other material you find, such as twigs, seashells, feathers, leaves, seaweed, cones and nut shells. It doesn't have to be big – just make it a size that feels right. You can also extend the S with more curves if you choose. The perfect time to make it is at the end of a walk, when you are feeling more relaxed. It is important to approach this practice from a calm place, rather than put any stress into the stones you choose.

The joy of this practice comes through the creative journey rather than the goal of completion. As you place each stone in the meandering S-shape, you get to slow down and feel each moment. You gently release worry and stress, just focusing on the texture of your finds and how they work together to create a piece of natural art.

Look for a few handfuls of small stones – and gather twigs, leaves and more to intersperse between the stones. Take your time gathering and placing your objects, and let your imagination flow. When your hands are busy, your creative, intuitive mind gets active because the left brain, which judges our thoughts, is occupied with the physical task. Tune in to what you are sensing and feeling.

Reflect on the S-shape you've created. You can simply sit with it, or you may find that you naturally interpret some of the stones or other finds as events in your life. Your S-shape might be soft and smooth in places and more jagged or angular in others.

When you are ready, dedicate your artwork as a gift to nature, and give thanks for your time here. Then deconstruct the path, giving the stones and other items back to the earth.

STONE RITUAL
Hag Stones for Visions

Hag stones, also known as witch stones, fairy stones and holey stones in British folklore, were portals to the fairy kingdom. They're defined as stones with a naturally formed hole that goes all the way through – so when you hold it up to the light you're looking through a tiny window. Hag stones may have one obvious hole or several, and are often found on beaches. The lore goes that if you look through a hag stone, you'll see fairies.

Whether you believe in fairies or not, you can work with a hag stone to engage with and explore your imagination. When you find a hag stone, look through it where you find it. With one eye closed, gaze through the hole or holes. Let your eyes relax and defocus, so your vision becomes misty. Rest for a moment and close your eyes. You may see images or get a strong knowing: this is inspiration from the creative self within.

If you do believe in fairies, it's thought that looking through a hag stone is a safe way to observe the little people without being enchanted by them (hence the stone's additional meaning of protection). The best times to see fairies are in the half-light between night and day – at dawn and dusk.

In the past, hag stones were threaded and hung round the neck to be worn as a charm, or placed on the horns of cattle, or hung on or near any person, animal or object that needed protection from curses. To promote fertility, a hag stone was tied to the marital bed. Today, you can use the charm as a shield against negative energy by wearing it as a pendant round your neck. Using a hag stone as a keyring protected property – the combination of iron and stone was believed to bring powerful protection.

STONE RITUAL
Making a Sun Charm for Optimism

The anthropologist James Frazer reported on a special custom of Banks Islanders in the Canadian arctic. Using owl feathers and a stone wound with red braid, the people made an image of the sun – a charm to make sunshine. An incantation was spoken as the charm was being made, and then it was hung from a high tree in a sacred place.

This ritual is adapted here as a charm for warmth, happiness and optimism. To make this charm is to bring in the light.

To make your own charm, find a round stone. As this is a sun charm, choose a warm, earthy colour, if available. Wind your stone with red braid (or long, strong grass, if you don't have red braid or cord). Make sure the winding is tight and secure, as you will need it to hold the feather shafts.

Using feathers you have found, push the shafts into the braid or grass, so that they radiate outward, like the rays of the sun.

Spend some time reflecting on your sun charm. You might ask yourself, "What can I be hopeful about? What can I focus on to bring me fulfilment?" Take it home if it's permitted and, if not, gently dismantle the charm (taking the red braid with you), after giving thanks.

8

Shells and Seaweed

Love and Home

Shells are symbols of love, sexuality, protection and the home. As physical protectors, shells encase what is vulnerable to attack. The shells we find on the beach are the afterlives of creatures of the sea – the little hard casings that once housed life. There's always a sense of departure and legacy: these often-beautiful specimens are what remains after the completion of a cycle. Shells' association with water and with women (some shells, such as the cowrie, represented female genitalia) suggest fertility and birth. Seaweed, like bird eggs, also holds the meaning of fertility and survival.

SEASHELL CHARMS

Shells can be bivalve (two joined shells) such as clams, mussels, oysters and scallops; or gastropods or univalves (single shell), such as abalone, snails and limpets. As with all other charms in this book, you don't need to be able to identify a shell to use it as a charm – although the symbolism of two (the bivalves) and one (the gastropod or univalve) can help shape the meaning you give it. Bivalves seem commonly associated with love, as of course they began life as two shells joined together, while the univalves are linked with money and confidence. A 1909 shell amulet on display at the Museum of Witchcraft and Magic in Cornwall, England, is made from an oyster shell. It is painted with two hearts, and a vertical arrow and letters – probably initials – appear within the hearts.

TRADITIONAL SHELL MEANINGS, QUALITIES AND USAGE

Below are the meanings, qualities and usage associated with a number of shells you may encounter on your seaside walks. This selection comes from a variety of cultural traditions.

Abalone, pearl oyster
Women, fertility, birth, love, the moon

Clam, mussel
Purification, love, good fortune

Conch
Communication, divinity

Cowrie
Fertility, prosperity, luck; in parts of Africa, cowries were bartered as small currency

Limpet
Courage, confidence, strength

Scallop
Fertility, baptism

SEAWEED CHARMS

Working with seaweed as a charm might seem off-putting at first, particularly if you are used to seeing heaps of kelp or bladderwrack piled up on the shoreline like debris. It's less daunting to look for smaller seaweed samples; collect a variety of colours and intricately shaped strands. You can dry or press them by placing them in some folded paper and putting them between a couple of large, heavy books. Or you could pick up one piece for luck or combine it with a shell for a love charm (see page 157).

Seaweed symbolizes nourishment, fertility and abundance. It's said that if you have seaweed in the house you will never be short of a friend – which may also refer to food as a "friend" in times of need.

One seaweed custom was related by a local woman in north-east England. As a child, she remembered that her grandfather always had seaweed hanging from the back of his kitchen door, which he used as a barometer. When the seaweed changed colour as it reacted to moisture in the air, it meant rain was on the way. Seaweed weather charms are still used in England to this day.

SEAWEED RITUAL
Seaweed and Wood to Send a Problem Away

In charm-work, water symbolizes moving on. You can give your problem to the water and find peace again – for example, you might choose to release a relationship, move home, or another issue that has drained you for too long. You will need access to flowing water. If you are by the sea or the ocean, you must check the local tide times. The charm is given to the sea on an outgoing tide to symbolize release.

Gather a piece of seaweed from the beach. If you are by a river, look on the riverbank for what the river has left behind, such as a small branch. The idea is that you take what the water has washed up – like wood and seaweed – and return it. Balance is then restored.

Get safely close to the water's edge and ask the water's permission to make a request. Be still and wait until you get a sign. This might be a dog's bark, the sudden cry of a gull or the wind changing direction. Or it may be more subtle than this – maybe you just sense that the sea or river is opening up to you.

Take your seaweed or wood and send your wish into it. Hold it and say:

"I ask that [this issue] be gone
Our time together is too long"

Then breathe on to the charm and say:

"Let peace and balance come to me
So mote it be."

Float the seaweed or wood on the water's surface. All you need do now is watch as the waves float your wish away and give thanks to the sea or the river.

SEASHELL RITUAL
A Seashell Love Charm

Beaches bring to mind romantic walks, dreams and the imagination. A beach walk is an opportunity to manifest what you want from a new relationship and/or to make a charm to confirm your wish to meet the right partner. You will need two seashells and some seaweed – look for string- or ribbon-like seaweed or otherwise choose sea grass, cord or thread.

As you walk the beach, think about the kind of relationship you would love to have.

Ask to find two shells for your charm. Scan the pebbles and stop when a shell calls to you. Pick it up, hold it and tune in to its energy. Sense if it feels right as a charm for love. You may end up with a bivalve, such as two joining mussel shells, or two that are quite different, but there will be something that attracts you to each one. Then let yourself daydream about your ideal partner. Focus on how you want to feel in the right relationship, rather than how your partner should look; charms get their power from emotion rather than ideals. Generate that feeling of love.

Hold the shells and gently wrap the seaweed or cord round them, joining them together, then make a knot to seal your intention. You can use a spoken charm if you prefer. I have not included one here, as this is such a personal request – and creating your own also helps you focus on your desire a little longer.

When your charm is finished, thank nature and carry your love charm with you, or add it to your altar. Light a candle on your altar before you display your charm there to signify lighting up or energizing your request for love.

TECHNIQUE
An Altar to the Sea

If you love the sea or the ocean, you can honour it with a sea altar. Bring together your beach treasures: pebbles, driftwood, sea grass, seaweed and sea glass (glass pounded smooth by the sea).

Collect a little sea water in a glass jar, with a little sand. You can arrange your finds as you like, or try grouping them by element. Representing the elements through natural charms signifies wholeness, as the four elements are the building blocks of the universe.

When you make an altar according to the elements, you remind yourself of the power of nature and how you are a part of it. Each element – earth, air, fire and water – has an associated compass direction:

Pebbles, sand and sea glass: Element of earth; place in the north of your altar

Sea grass: Element of air; place in the east of your altar

Driftwood: Element of fire; place in the south of your altar

Water jar and seaweed: Element of water; place in the west of your altar

You can go to your altar whenever you need perspective – when you feel caught up in detail and need help stepping back. Contemplating your altar charms often brings a sense of peace and balance, as what you see is whole.

TECHNIQUE
Pressing Seaweed

Seaweed holds the memories of the seas and oceans. Researchers have recently discovered that levels of nitrogen in historical seaweed tissues echoed changes in currents and the climate from over one hundred years ago.[24]

Queen Victoria and many other women of her era embraced the popularity of natural history through "seaweeding", (gathering seaweed). The results are beautiful; up close, you can see the colour and delicacy of miniature trees that were once in motion.

1. Gather a selection of damp seaweed, aiming for small amounts of different varieties.
2. Wash, then press them in an old newspaper, using tweezers to separate out any delicate fronds first.
3. Sandwich them between cardboard and top with heavy weights, such as bricks or tiles.
4. Leave them for at least a week to dry, but check after two or so days as some weeds dry out quickly; they will soon be ready to frame or place on your altar as a tribute to the sea.

9

Eggshells and Feathers

Transformation, Wishes and Blessings

Eggshells are symbols of transformation, and in folk tales, they seem aligned with unwanted fairy folk and bad witches. In the Celtic story *Brewery of Eggshells*, a mother believes her baby is enchanted because he is skeletal and cannot grow. When she boils 12 eggshells, her baby suddenly tells her he is 1500 years old and has never before seen a brew made of eggshells – confirmation that her baby has been changed into a fairy. She is told she must kill him with a hot poker, but she slips on the floor. The old fairy spirit is banished, and the child survives. By throwing out the eggs and cooking up the shells (rather than boiling eggs the usual way) the mother performed a kind of reverse magic, which breaks the fairy curse.

In a Welsh version of the tale collected by Joseph Jacobs[25], a mother must heat some potage in a hen's eggshell, ostensibly for the reapers, and stand with it at the door near her bewitched twin babies. If the babies gurgled as usual all was well, but they began to speak:

"Acorn before oak I knew,
An egg before a hen,
But I never heard of an eggshell brew
A dinner for harvest men."

The mother throws the enchanted babies in the lake, where goblins swap them for her true children. This reciprocity is echoed in the custom of children putting their milk teeth under the pillow for the tooth fairy. If the tooth fairy came that night, she would leave a silver sixpence or other gift under the child's pillow in exchange for the teeth.

Eggshells also seem to be a favourite of witches, as witches supposedly used them for destructive sympathetic magic – making eggshells stand in for ships at sea. When they destroyed the eggshell, they wrecked the ship. An echo of this unwarranted belief is the custom of destroying an eggshell after eating the egg so witches could not use them for their dark deeds. This ritual is still practised in England today.

When it came to fairies and eggshells, it seems fairies simply preferred them as retreats, and had no plans to use them to terrify humans. Folklorist Francesca Wilde relates: *"Egg shells are favourite retreats of the fairies, therefore the judicious eater should always break the shell after use, to prevent the fairy sprite from taking up his lodgement therein."*[26]

A Wish for Change

If you find an empty eggshell, take a small piece of it to add to your herb pouch (see pages 118–119). The shell piece grants a wish for change.

FEATHER SYMBOLISM

Feathers are symbols of prayers and wishes – the hope that a desire will manifest. In the Grimm tale *The Three Feathers*, an old king must decide which of his three sons will inherit the kingdom. He tells his sons that the one who brings back a beautiful carpet will win the crown. To start them off on their quest, the king blows three feathers into the air and commands, "You shall go as they fly." Eventually, after a number of further tests, the youngest son – the underdog – wins the competition, because he followed a feather that settled on the ground. While sitting mournfully next to it, he spied a trap door leading to a wish-granting toad who gave him everything his father asked for. The feathers represent the king's wishes, manifested through his youngest son.

Feathers represent the power of the element of air – mind and thought, freedom and spirit – and take on the meaning of birds, those celestial messengers who traverse Earth and heaven. Nordic god Odin kept two ravens named Huginn ("thought") and Muninn ("memory"), who acted as informers, bringing Odin news from Earth to Asgard, the realm of the gods. Feathers also signify messages from loved ones in spirit and the angels; seeing a white feather in an unexpected place can be confirmation from angels that you are on the right path. In folklore, a white feather is a lucky omen.

"Feathers represent the power of the element of air – mind and thought, freedom and spirit."

Feathers from birds with dark or black feathers are associated with magic, divination and protection. Crows and ravens in particular were seen as magical messengers of the gods. In Welsh mythology, the raven was sacred to Bran (meaning "crow" or "raven"), a giant of a man and one-time king of Britain. When dying, he prophesised that if his followers cut off his head and carried it around with them they would have 80 years of entertainment, as his head would still be able to talk (it was believed that the head was the seat of the soul). The prophecy came true, and the followers had 80 years without any sense of time passing. Bran's head was finally buried at the Tower of London, which is famously inhabited by ravens who are reputed to protect the Tower and the country.

FEATHER RITUAL
Feathers for Confidence

In this practice, we make a charm using two feathers – one to represent luck and the other for security and protection. The idea is that we generate luck through positive thought and action, but that we need to do so within safe boundaries – hence the need for protection. This is the perfect charm to make when you are about to take a decision involving a risk and need to feel confident that you are making the right choice.

On your walk (or over several walks, if it takes you longer to find the feathers), gather a white or light-coloured feather and a black or dark feather. Bind the feathers together with grass or another stem and tie a knot. Dedicate your charm by asking it to work with you and repeating out loud three times your purpose or wish.

Then give thanks and carry it with you. When you no longer need your feather charm, untie the knot and leave the charm in nature, again with gratitude.

FEATHER RITUAL
Feathers for Inspiration

As feathers were used as quills, there's a sympathetic connection between feathers, writing and other forms of creative communication. When you need ideas, display some found feathers in a pot or vase on your altar or place where you write or do other creative work – on your desk or dining table, for example, or a table in a room in which you like to read, relax and dream.

Choose long, strong feathers – these will be from the wing or tail of the bird, but don't worry if you can't identify your feathers as such. Do it by eye: pick those that look and feel firm, with a solid "flight" (the central stem or quill). These feathers help the bird to fly, and they can help your ideas fly, too.

FEATHER RITUAL
A Feather Wishing Bottle

A feather wishing bottle is simply a feather in a charm bottle you can carry or wear round your neck. It's a visible reminder of a wish, helping you stay connected with your positive intentions for the future.

Charm bottles come with a stopper, so you can place a small feather within it – these will be the fluffy down or contour feathers. The feather symbolizes your wish.

First of all, what will you wish for? Reflect on what you need, and if this will make you happy. It is best not to ask directly for money, as this sets up poverty consciousness – an awareness of what you lack rather than what you have.

> "What will you wish for? Reflect on what you need, and if this will make you happy."

Visualize your wish coming true and play it out like a movie. See it happening and generate lots of positive emotion around it.

Speak your wish aloud to activate the charm. It's best to write out your wish first, keeping it as simple as possible, then recite it. At the end, say: "Thank you for my wish come true."

Then, trust that what you need will come to you. Do not think too much about it afterwards: you have put positive energy into your future and that is enough.

The final step is to recognize your granted wish when it comes. If we're too narrow about our expectations, we limit what we see. Abundance may come to you as money, but it may come as much-needed help. Whatever you receive, say thank you, unconditionally (rather than, "Thank you, but that's not what I ordered."). When you receive with grace, that opens the door to more. Resistance sets up blocks to receiving.

All there is to do now is wear your wish bottle for as long as you need to.

Feather Alternative

As an alternative, use dandelion seeds in place of feathers, as dandelion puff-balls also hold the meaning of wishes (see page 109).

TRADITIONAL FEATHER COLOUR MEANINGS

If you find a feather of the colour listed below, you can dedicate it as a charm according to its meaning. (Note that feathers of some colours will be harder to find than others.) Of course, it would be rare to see a bright yellow or purple feather on your travels, but look closely for delicate colour hues. For example, if you picked a black feather and on closer inspection noticed a purple sheen, you'd look up the meaning of both black and purple in the list below.

White: Ask for luck, angelic guidance, or a sign from a recently departed loved one

Black: Request protection, or ask for self-connection and intuitive power

Black and white: Ask for change or help with making a decision that brings change

Orange: Wish for inspiration and motivation to reach goals

Blue: Ask that you see the truth, and/or gain a broader perspective

Grey: Wish for peace and calm

Yellow: Request clarity, warmth and insight

Purple: Wish for deeper understanding and spiritual knowledge

Green: Ask for abundance, healing and success

Brown: Wish for some rewarding time at home or to feel secure or to stay grounded

Red: Request love, passion and vitality

Pink: Wish for new friends, or nurturing honest, caring relationships

Iridescence: Ask for the ability to discern, to see through artifice

TRADITIONAL BIRD SYMBOLISM

In many cultures and belief systems, birds were regarded as sacred messengers who communicated with deities. Because they fly through the air, birds naturally gained the meaning of communication and spiritual knowledge. Native American tribes revered the eagle as a two-way communicator between human and god and a symbol of strength and wisdom, while the augurs of ancient Rome interpreted bird behaviour as the will of the gods.

Blackbird

Mystery, endings, transformation

Crow

Wisdom, the shadow self, courage, transformation, magic

Dove, pigeon

Peace, love, family, communication

Duck

Opportunities, resources, comfort

Eagle

Strength, leadership, vision, wisdom, inspiration, success

Goldfinch

Joy in life, freedom, resurrection

Goose

Finding direction, loyalty, prosperity, synchronicity

Gull

Optimism, action, enjoyment

Hawk

Memory, decisions, connecting with ancestors

Hummingbird

Infinity symbol, going with the flow, freedom, luck

Ibis
Creativity, wisdom

Jay
Vitality, determination, intelligence, faithfulness

Magpie
Ingenuity, intelligence, news, opportunism, sociability

Owl
Intuition, wisdom, psychic work

Peacock
Abundance, purity, success

Pheasant
Attraction, passion, creativity

Raven
Wisdom, prophecy, spiritual messages, intelligence, news

Robin
Sign from a loved one in spirit

Sparrow
Strength, community

Swallow
Acuity, bravery, comfort, renewal

Swan
Protection, fidelity, partnership, love, grace

Swift
Opportunity, realizing potential

Warbler
Freedom, dance, music, self-expression

Wren
Courage, motivation, wisdom, lightness of spirit

PART THREE

Going Deeper

Making art in nature is a life-affirming practice, celebrating our time in the wild and the beauty of what we find. When we create the sacred shapes and symbols in this part, we harness the energy of ancient templates to empower our meditation practice, energize creative projects and connect with guidance. We learn how to investigate the shape of the charms we've chosen, as well as the shapes that occur to us in the landscape – in clouds, reflections in water, the pattern of sand and so on. We also delve into the meanings of sacred shapes and symbols by examining numbers as stages of growth, focusing particularly on the magical numbers 3, 6, 9 and 7 in charm-work.

10

Sacred Shapes and Symbols

Nature's Art

The sacred shapes featured in this chapter are the mandala, circle, spiral, vesica piscis, tree, pentagram and infinity symbol. All have provenance and power, and are simple to recreate with natural charms on your altar or outdoors. When in nature, you can also enter the magical spirit of the form by walking a symbol or drawing it in the earth as part of your ritual.

"Many people feel a sense of peace and balance when making nature art, because they're allowing their whole selves to take part in the activity. There's balance between the conscious and unconscious mind, the logical and the imaginal."

THE APPROACH:
DISCOVERY AND BELONGING

When making art in nature, the aim is to work gently and mindfully. The goal is not to have the perfect design. Rather, the purpose is the journey and appreciating texture, shape and colour in unique combinations – for example, what you discover while choosing and positioning your finds in a pattern; which leaves, petals, shells, stones and feathers go together and so on.

It is natural to become immersed in what you're doing, and almost impossible to be anywhere else in your mind, as you focus purely on the charms you hold and the design that begins to unfold.

Working with your hands gives your thinking mind a break. A physical activity distracts the thoughts that rush to assess and judge, making internal space for the intuitive part of you to rise. For this reason, many people feel a sense of peace and balance when making nature art, because they're allowing their whole selves to take part in the activity. There's balance between the conscious and unconscious mind, the logical and the imaginal.

But there is another reason that natural art benefits the soul: when you create a sacred shape in nature, you set up a circuit of relationships, as every part of every shape has a role in creating the whole. As the maker, you are also part of this web of connection – you enter the spirit of the form and become part of it. You belong.

SACRED SHAPES RITUAL
Making a Freestyle Mandala

A mandala is a symbol of wholeness and the cycle of life. A nature mandala comprises a pattern of natural objects that represents the wholeness of earth through its materials: wood, stone, plant matter, feather, shells. Mandala designs are usually symmetrical, and many are wheel-like with concentric rings. This ritual makes a freestyle mandala, beginning only with a central point. The rest of the design is up to you, and will naturally develop during the making.

You'll need to select one item for the centre of your design to act as a focal point. This might be a shell, a feather, a pine cone, a moss-covered root or a nut – whatever you feel drawn to at this moment. Begin by placing your focal object in position, then, working from the centre outward, lay down your items. As you position each piece, use your senses to tell you if it's in the right place. Feel free to move them around until they, and you, feel settled and you're happy with the result.

When you're ready, stand away from your design and appreciate what you have created. The finished mandala may form a particular shape or pattern that holds meaning for you. You may feel that you've chosen certain colours and shapes to express an unconscious idea or need. Equally, your mandala may not suggest anything other than itself. Any response is perfect, as there's no goal. You will have noticed fresh and beautiful detail in your finds – in leaf stems and serrations, the fine sheen of a chalky pebble or the way the light catches the sun-like head of a dandelion flower.

When you have finished, take a moment to appreciate your art. Spend a minute or two gazing into the centre of your creation, to enter the mandala and journey through the lines and shapes you see in this unique combination of finds. This is your time for self-reflection – a memory, an idea or a message may come to you.

When you're ready, dismantle the mandala, working from the outside in. If possible, put the pieces back where you found them, then give thanks and walk on.

Putting together random pieces to create a new whole is an act of healing. If you see the pieces as parts of life, the mandala connects them in a new way; they look different now. You may feel you gain a new perspective on the past and present.

"Accepting that you made art in the moment and are willing to let it go also means your memory of it is perfect."

Deconstructing your mandala might feel difficult at first. But our role here is to leave everything as we found it, to leave no trace of our visit. Accepting that you made art in the moment and are willing to let it go also means your memory of it is perfect. Keep that memory and look forward to what you can create on your next walk.

TECHNIQUE
Collecting Finds

You'll need to collect around 20 pieces, depending on the size of your symbol – you can work with the little finds you've already gathered along your walk, or you can plan ahead and bring along some charms gathered on previous walks. To create a pattern, you will need charms that are similar and contrasting. You might choose, say, six small leaves of the same type and six petals, along with a handful of mixed bark, seeds, stones or feathers to create textural interest. Overall, though, opt for what feels right. Go with your senses and your body when deciding what to use and what to leave out.

You may choose to create your work on one theme – a ring of deep green ivy leaves, a ring of furled birch leaves, with a beautiful red autumnal leaf as your centrepiece; or you could make a feather mandala, using feather-down and a selection of feathers you find nearby. It's also liberating to experiment by adding in more elements. You may be drawn to make further shapes in or around the original shape. If so, keep going, keep creating. You can take photographs of the many stages your art goes through as a reminder of your time in this special place.

Find a space to lay out your finds that isn't too windy – a sheltered and, ideally, level area. A beach on an outgoing tide is perfect, as you can gently press your finds into semi-wet sand to keep them stable as you make your symbol. In woodland, you might find a flattish area of damp earth, or go to a sheltered spot in your garden. A garden table, patio, balcony, terrace or lawn may be just right, too.

Nature art is intended to be temporary – we focus on creating it then, when finished, walk away. Rather than take the pieces home, you give everything back to nature as a gesture of respect and thanks.

SACRED SHAPES RITUAL
Making a Group Mandala

As a group ritual, mandala-making is a perfect way to end a charm-walk. You can do this with two or more people, with each person contributing their charm-finds. Plan this for a certain time – such as on a waning moon, for releasing the old; on a new moon, for bringing in new energies and opportunities; or on an equinox, to welcome in a new cycle or season.

1. Aim to make a joint decision about what to use as the central object – or decide to use more than one, if each person wants to contribute. The only guidance here is not to move any pieces that another person has placed in the mandala and to let the mandala grow organically.
2. You may talk as you work, or work in silence. If you begin talking, you'll often find that chatter soon recedes as each of you becomes immersed in the project.
3. When you have finished, stand together in a circle round the mandala. Each person either makes a personal wish for the future, which can be private or shared with the group, or just takes a moment for reflection. It often happens that the group naturally separates when the weather changes – a shift in the light or wind direction tells us when it's time to move on.
4. Give thanks to nature, then replace the finds, gently dismantling the mandala.

SACRED SHAPES RITUAL
Walking the Circle for
Release or Manifestation

The circle, symbol of the earth, represents commitment, connectedness and wholeness. It also signifies protection, as its boundary is continuous: inside a circle, we feel secure.

In this ritual, you walk the circle (by literally walking in a circle) to connect with the spirit of the form, and in so doing either release an issue or make a wish.

First, look for a sheltered area with enough space to walk – you will need room for around three to five paces or so. Work with a friend to practise this ritual if you tend to feel self-conscious on your own: when you walk the circle you need to feel relaxed and safe. Tune in to the energy here; connect with the spirit of place (see pages 51–55). Reflect on what you need to release or banish from your life, or what you want to invite in.

Pythagoreans expressed the concept of divine intelligence as a circle with a central dot. Walking a circle round a central stone or feather echoes this ancient symbol.

WALKING THE CIRCLE FOR RELEASE

Find a small stone that resonates with you. Connect with it by tuning in to it (see Chapter 7) and ask it to ground your request and protect you throughout the ritual. Place it in a central position. Now imagine in your mind's eye the space for the circle round the stone before you walk it (if you find it difficult to visualize, you can mark out some points of the circle with small stones as a guide). Physically walk slowly anticlockwise while you think about what you want to release. How will you feel without this burden? Give it to the earth as you walk the circle three times – the stone will ground your request.

WALKING THE CIRCLE FOR MANIFESTATION

Find a feather to represent your wishes. Connect with it by holding it and tuning in to it, then push it into the earth so it stands upright. Visualize a circle round it. Now physically walk clockwise to bring in something new – think it and wish it, and feel how you will feel when it happens. Generate these feelings as if it is already done. Walk round in your circle slowly three times in total. As you walk, the feather transmits your wish. When you have finished, give thanks and remove your stone or feather, taking it with you or leaving it behind in a suitable place, as you prefer.

SACRED SHAPES RITUAL
The Spiral – Sacred
Geometry for Meditation

Sacred geometry in nature refers to the organic shape, proportion and growth patterns in the natural world: think of the spiral of the nautilus shell or the pine cone, the perfect comma of an unfurling fern, the pattern of an artichoke or the seeds in a sunflower. It's all down to the Fibonacci sequence – a formula of accumulation that explains why plants grow in a particular way; when mapped onto a chart, the rising numbers create a spiral.

"This practice helps you slow down and enjoy the journey rather than focusing on completion."

When you recreate a spiral, you celebrate life: your charm spiral echoes the organizing principle of the universe. You can make a small spiral for your altar, using a selection of charms, or create it out in nature. The benefit of this ritual is to work slowly and mindfully, so give yourself time to collect your finds together, and to place each stone one by one. You will need about a dozen charms or more, depending on the size of your spiral.

Here we are not manifesting anything, nor making any request. The meditation is the whole process – gathering leaves, twigs, stones, cones, shells, seeds, flowers, feathers and more, and laying them in the spiral shape. The physical action of placing the charms brings you into the present moment. It helps to work with the breath: breathe in as you hold an item and exhale as you place it. Then breathe naturally for a moment or two before you repeat for the next item. This practice helps you slow down and enjoy the journey rather than focusing on completion. The sense of physical expansion creates mental space – and that feeling that you are right here, right now.

When you are ready to end your meditation, stand back from your spiral and appreciate what you have created. Then dismantle it, working from the outside in, replacing your finds (or taking them with you, if allowed). Give thanks to nature and to yourself for making time to do this.

SACRED SHAPES RITUAL
Vesica Piscis for Creativity

Vesica piscis signifies life, fertility and creativity. Comprising two overlapping circles, the term is Latin for "bladder of a fish" – most fish have two air bladders – which suggests the dual shape. The intersecting circles form an almond shape, which is known as a mandorla (meaning "almond") and can be seen as a vulva, hence the meaning of fertility and life. The whole symbol is sometimes referred to as the "womb of the Universe", as other geometric shapes can be created within it – the triangle, rhombus, square, rectangle, pentagon and hexagon. As everything comes from vesica piscis, it's a powerful form to work with when you need to raise energy for creative projects and bring in new relationships.

You can construct the vesica piscis indoors on your altar, or out in nature. To begin, think about which natural charms you feel drawn to use. One approach is to gather those that have a natural almond shape – flower petals, leaves such as those of the bay laurel, beech

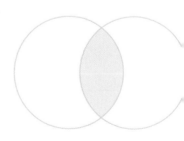

or cherry, and seeds like sunflower or pumpkin. But, as ever, go with what feels right for you.

The form of the vesica piscis creates energy, and your intention activates it. Think carefully about how you would like your project or relationship to grow, and visualize this happening as you work. Dedicate your vesica piscis to your wish by asking it to work with you and repeating out loud three times your purpose or desire, and give thanks.

Make one circle of charms, then create the second circle so it's positioned half-way across the first one, creating the central mandorla. In the mandorla, place something that represents your creative work or a relationship you would like to nurture. For example, you might choose a budding twig for a project, or a flower head or heart-shaped leaf to represent a person. If you work with crystals, place a crystal here – for example, a clear quartz to magnify your wish, a rose quartz for love or a citrine for abundance. Placing these items in the mandorla creates a visual focus of your wish.

If you're sensitive to moon cycles, you can make your vesica piscis on a new moon, which supports growth and expansion.

If you are outside, dismantle the symbol, giving your finds back to nature or taking them with you if permitted. If you make the vesica piscis on your home altar, take it down when you feel your charms' work is done.

Bracelet Alternative

As an alternative you could make two vine bracelets – follow the instructions on page 139. Place them on your altar in the vesica piscis shape, so they're overlapping. As above, add a symbol of your intention in the central mandorla.

SACRED SHAPES RITUAL
The Tree for Growth and Family

The shape of the tree is one of the primary forms found in nature – naturally, in the trees themselves, but in other plants and places, too. Cut a red cabbage in half and discover the tree hiding inside it; or look at the frost on a window pane, frozen trees form like winter ghosts, a reminder of new life to come after the thaw.

In this practice, you can create a temporary tree indoors and photograph it when you are finished – this may take you an hour or more – or you can make your tree out in nature, which you can do more quickly. Making the tree is a meditation on life and the connections we make during our time here on Earth. The tree represents family – hence the idea of family trees. With the oldest ancestor placed at the top and younger family members on the lowest branches, we remember that life is progression, and the tree represents the journey through birth, death and rebirth. You may wish to make your tree a family tree or a friendship tree or even a family tree that represents your chosen rather than biological family. In a broader sense, your tree can be an affirmation of life and growth for all.

It is best to work on a table rather than your altar, as you will need room to spread out. You'll also need to place a background under your charms, such as ironed fabric or a large piece of paper or board.

When placing your charms to form the tree shape, aim for balance. Traditional tree-of-life symbols have the same spread of roots and branches, as if the lower half of the tree were a mirror-image of the upper half. This expresses the idea of balance in nature and also the maxim "As above, so below", which means that all things are connected as one.

As you arrange your charms, focus on this idea of connection. You'll begin to see new details in the twigs, feathers, herbs, grasses, stones and moss you might choose, and notice similarities and differences between these materials when they're placed side by side. On the branches you can represent your family or your friends with the same type of charm – for example, maybe all oak leaves or small feathers. Alternatively, add in small photographs of your people or small tokens that remind you of them. A shell might represent a friend who loves being by the sea; a feather might signify a relative who loves to write; or you could use a piece of jewellery, or their initial or name written on a slip of paper.

When you are finished, don't rush to take your photograph. Rest with the image for a while. Take it into your mind's eye and see where it leads you. Memories may come to you, or other information from your own well of knowing.

RITUAL
Making Your Tree Outdoors – the 30-minute Ritual

To make your tree outdoors, find a sheltered, flat space where you won't be disturbed. You'll need to choose a time when it's not windy, so your charms won't easily scatter. Ideally, press your finds into damp earth or sand to temporarily fix them in place – again, this helps if an unexpected gust comes along.

You can use charms you've brought with you or those you find on the spot. For example, you can create the tree trunk with a handful of stones and make the branches using fallen branch pieces, twigs and leaves from different trees to add colour and contrast. Improvise with what you have, and you'll find that you work quite quickly. Being in nature often gives you fresh inspiration and ideas, too, so your design might go in unexpected directions.

Spend some time – weather permitting – reflecting on your artwork before taking your photograph. If you're not in your own yard or garden, dismantle the tree before you leave.

SACRED SHAPES RITUAL
The Pentagram for Protection

The pentagram is an ancient symbol that has held many meanings – the human body, the five senses, the union of male and female and nature's elements (earth, air, fire and water, with spirit, the top point of the star, as the overseer); it has been associated with loyalty, perfection and luck, and today is widely associated, in Wiccan tradition, with magic and protection. In all, its unequal number of points represents the synthesis of different energies as one powerful force.

To begin, look for five pieces of wood to make the pentagram shape. It's not just practical – trees themselves represent the four elements of nature plus the fifth element of spirit. Its wood is burned for fire, its leaves (which signify earth) float in the air, and its surfaces collect water. The upper branches, reaching to the sky, signify the fifth element of spirit.

"Just as cooks are warned never to cook when angry, always craft your charms when you're in a good place emotionally and physically."

You can make your pentagram indoors or outdoors. Outdoors is ideal, as you benefit from the relaxed feeling of connection that comes with being close to the earth. If it's not practical to work outside, as this project can take some time, work indoors in a quiet room with plenty of light. Just as cooks are warned never to cook when angry, always craft your charms when you're in a good place emotionally and physically.

Cut your twigs or small branches to roughly the same length, then lay them out in the shape of an upright five-pointed star, with a single point at the top and two points at the bottom. Using twine, string or vine, bind the twigs together at the ends, then tie the twigs that cross over each other near the centre. Finish each tie with a knot, sealing in your wish (see Chapter 6). If you wish, you can add in other finds, too, weaving in small feathers, moss, fronds of fern or ivy and brightly coloured leaves.

When your pentagram is finished, display it upright (with one point at the top) on or above your altar space or wherever feels right to you. As a spiritual symbol of protection, the pentagram shields you from negative energy entering your home if you hang it above the front door, and it guards the room if you place it above an internal door.

SACRED SHAPES RITUAL
Infinity for Decisions

The infinity or sideways figure of eight symbol represents the concept of endlessness and cosmic balance. The line flows eternally in the shape of two connected and equal loops, a number eight on its side. Eight is the number of renewal, as seen in the octagonal baptismal font. The infinity symbol dominates the Two of Pentacles card in the most popular tarot card deck, the Rider-Waite-Smith deck. These cards were first published in 1909 by Rider, conceived by leading occultist A E Waite and illustrated by Pamela Colman Smith. On the Two of Pentacles, a man wields a huge infinity symbol, unsure of which path to take. In this practice, we create the infinity symbol to meditate on a decision. One loop of the symbol represents one option, and the other loop signifies the other option.

You will need to be able to access mud, sand, gravel or snow – a surface on which you can draw the shape. If this isn't possible, make the symbol with two leaves (see below).

First, find a twig, a branch or some driftwood, and then a sheltered space. Rest for a moment and tune in to the land, feeling open to what you may see, hear, smell and feel here, at this moment. Take your stick and practise tracing the infinity symbol in the air. Begin at the centre, go left and up to make the left loop, then right and up to make the right loop, finishing in the centre. Now repeat and use your breath – try breathing in as you make the left loop and breathing out as you make the right one.

When you are ready, take your stick and draw the symbol in the ground, using the same breathing technique. When you breathe the shape, you bring it into your consciousness – and it becomes active. (If you're using leaves, gather two leaves that have a teardrop shape. Put them on the ground so the leaf-points are touching in the middle, to make the figure of eight shape.) Imagine that one loop is Option A and the other loop is Option B.

Follow the shape with your gaze as many times as you like, letting the symbol flow into your mind. When you feel ready to stop, finish by resting your eyes on the central point, where the lines of the shape intersect in the centre or the leaves touch. Close your eyes and go inward at this point of pure balance. Ask your question: "Shall I do this or this?" Or, "What's the best option now?" The answer you need will come to you intuitively.

You can also practise this at home with a pen and paper. Draw the symbol and assign an option to each loop. For example, the left-hand loop could mean "stay" and the right-hand loop could mean "go", or "yes" and "no". Take a breath and begin to trace over the shape continually. Have your eyes half-closed as you do this, so you can see where the pen is going but you're not acutely aware of the detail. After a time, stop. Look at the loops: the loop that is bolder or denser is your answer.

SACRED SHAPES RITUAL
The Bow for Love

A bow, with its dual loop, represents marriage and commitment. Making a bow charm is a simple as tying a shoelace, and you can make several bows for your altar or charm tree depending on what you would like your bow to attract. One bow stands for finding a new relationship. Two bows stand for togetherness, while three gives a new relationship wings; four is for stability and five is for faithfulness (see Chapter 11 for more numbers and their meanings).

To make your bows, you can use vine from a climbing plant, or other organic material you can easily bend, such as grass or corn. If you don't have that to hand, make your bows with red braid or ribbon (red energizes your love wish). When you tie the bow, mentally send your wish into it.

For example, to wish for a new relationship with someone you've just met, you can say:

"Me (make the first loop)
And you (make the second loop)
A new love true (tie the bow)
So mote it be."
(or "Amen" or "Thank you" if you prefer)

To strengthen an existing relationship, make two bows for your altar or charm tree. When you make each bow, you can say:

"Me (make the first loop)
And you (make the second loop)
Forever true". (tie the bow)

Of course, you can make up your own words – do whatever feels right for you.

Make the bows on a new moon, so your wish will be delivered by the full moon.

TECHNIQUE
Recreating the Original

As sympathetic magic is based on imitating an "original", one further way to create art with your charms is to use the shape of your charm's source.

So, if you have wood or nut charms, use them to create the tree symbol. With feathers, create a pair of wings. If you have seashells, make a larger shell, or three wavy lines to represent water. With fallen, empty eggshells, create a nest or a bird. A selection of petals from different varieties of flower can come together to make one unique flowerhead.

When you make art that recreates the original, you are honouring the source of your charms, which is nature herself.

This practice reminds you where your charms have come from, bringing you closer to nature – particularly on days when you can't get outdoors. Art, as they say, imitates life.

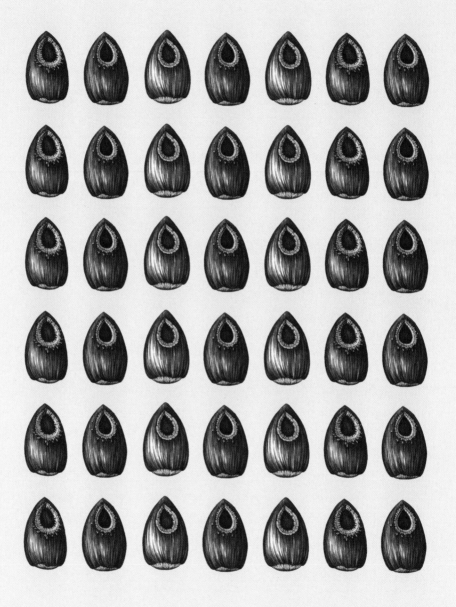

11

Magical Number Meanings

When you become symbol-aware, you may find that you begin to notice certain shapes, as if unconsciously reeling in a repeat image. When this happens, it means a particular shape has special meaning for you. One way to access this meaning is through the shape's "number" – this is simply its number of sides, or the number of charms you find naturally clustered together in one place.

NUMBER AS LIVING ENERGY

In ancient cultures, numbers had distinct character traits and were often believed to be living energies with the power to affect people's lives. The Aztecs believed numbers were good or evil, and were associated with the gods, along with particular colours and compass directions. Thirteen, for example, was a sacred number – there are 13 heavens in Aztec mythology, and the Aztec week was 13 days. Thirteen was therefore associated with endings and beginnings, a meaning echoed in the tarot's Death card, numbered 13, which stands for the completion of one cycle and the beginning of the next.

Chinese numerology is practised in feng shui, the ancient geomantic art that helps good energy flow in homes and landscapes. The Lo Shu square is a feng shui tool – the square is a magic number grid that contains the numbers 1 to 9. Each row, column and diagonal adds up to the same number: 15. (Fifteen is significant because it represents the number of days from the new moon to the full moon.) The square is placed over a floorplan of a building or an area of land. The feng shui practitioner can divine the fortune of the building, the land and the person by interpreting the numbers: each has an associated compass direction, element, colour and even a gender.

"To Pythagoras, numbers represented a force, an energy that explained the patterning and proportions we see in nature."

Pythagorean number theory, named after the sixth-century BCE Greek philosopher and mathematician Pythagoras, saw numbers as the organizing principle of the universe. The one, or divine intelligence, births the two, which produces the three, and so on. To Pythagoras, numbers represented a force, an energy that explained the patterning and proportions we see in nature – from the coil of a seashell to the perfect repeat motif of a pineapple fruit.

NOTICING YOUR PERSONAL SHAPES

We notice pattern in nature because nature is pattern. Walk in nature, and you become subtly attuned to a certain shape or pattern. It's as if the pattern of a leaf vein or the dewy lines of a spider's web sings out to us, and somewhere in our depths we listen and respond. We carry its song as we walk along and, because like attracts like, we begin to sense the pattern in one place, then another. We tune in to the wavelength. Say, for example, you pick up a pine cone, and you notice its long, triangular form made by the three sides. You're then drawn to three-leaved clovers, then triangular markings in tree bark, as the shape leads you onward.

Reflecting on one walk, I saw how I'd been drawn to circles – first to the circles on the trunk of a silver birch tree, then to the circular head of a daisy and on to the globe shape of a dandelion puff-ball. I didn't consciously choose circles on my walk, but they were there, in the stream of the unconscious, asking for attention. Later, I meditated on the circle, visualizing it in my mind's eye. What unfolded then was the message that a situation was now complete. I'd been thinking I had more to do on a project, considering making yet more revisions. The circle suggested that the work was done, and it was time to let it go. Circles take the meaning of the number 1, which is unity (see page 211).

Each shape listed overleaf has a corresponding number that offers a path to further interpretation. These number meanings are intended as starting points, a spark for your intuition and imagination, rather than rules to go by.

DIVINING YOUR CHARM'S NUMBER

Your charm relates to a number according to its form. You can divine a number for your charm by its overall shape or by the number of features it has. For example, this may be the number of petals on a flower or the number of buds on a branch. Go with whatever is most obvious: rather than count the multiple flower heads on a stem of geranium, go with the circle – the obvious shape of the whole.

If you have a compound leaf – for example, lots of oval leaves branching from one vein – you can go by the shape of the individual leaves, the shape of the whole leaf, or the number of leaves on the stem. Choose one and look up that number or look up all three.

The shape profiles also include the shapes you notice in the landscape, from waves to rainbows to birds and insects.

SHAPE AND ASSOCIATED NUMBER

Find the shape of your object in the descriptions below, then refer to the number meanings on pages 211–216.

Circle, Ring and Oval

Number 1. The circle and oval shapes have one continual line, and are associated with the number 1. Find the circle or oval in shells such as the limpet and cowrie, seed pods such as the cypress, poppy or gum tree; in the sphere of the dandelion puff-ball, clover flower or sea urchin; in the oval shape of acorns; in round leaves like those of the beech; and in berries, wild mushrooms and evenly rounded stones.

If you resonate with the circle today on your walk, you may also notice it in the loops of tree branches, the concentric rings of a felled tree-trunk, the sun and the moon; or in a reflected rainbow, and in spiders' webs and fairy rings. Fairy rings, those fabled portals to fairyland, appear in grass as dark green circles or as rings of toadstools.

Spiral

Numbers 1 and 6. The spiral has one continuous line, so it relates to number 1, and it also resembles the number 6. See this in the curl of a fern, a coiled seashell or snail shell, and in the growth pattern of plants such as the cactus. When you look into a rose, you will see that the petals form in a spiral shape.

You may also see the spiral at the beach, in the curl of waves as they form and crest, and in eddies in rivers; in vapour trails in the sky; and even in the flight pattern of insects when you notice how a moth spirals round the night light in your yard or garden.

Infinty Symbol (Figure of 8)

Naturally, this shape takes the number 8. You might see this symbol in the loops of grapevines, beanstalks or ivy.

If the figure of 8 is important to you today, you may also see it in the flight pattern of birds and insects, whorls on tree trunks and in the form of criss-crossing tree branches.

Almond

A shape with two sides relates to number 2. See this in the almond shape of tree leaves and petals, such as bluebell leaves and daisy petals, and the shape of peach stones (pits).

You'll also find it in eye-shaped markings on tree trunks.

Heart Shape

The heart relates to the triangle and number 3. It includes heart-shaped leaves such as the clover, ivy and lilac leaves and some palm leaves; you might find it in the form of a wild strawberry, a stone or a pebble on the seashore.

Elsewhere, the heart appears in cloud formations, puddles and reflections: when the swan dips its beak into water, its reflection makes the shape of a heart.

Cone and Triangle

The cone takes the number 3 or 1, depending on its shape – if it's sphere-like, it is number 1 and if more triangular, it takes number 3. Or, if you're drawn to the spiral pattern, go for number 6. This shape is seen in pine cones, the seed head of cone flowers, and in the shape of whelk, cone and conch shells.

In the wider environment, see the cone in the shape of trees and in landscape features such as hills, mountains, boulders and termite mounds.

Square and Oblong

Number 4. This shape is found less frequently in nature, but you may see it in stones and in markings on bark. It's sometimes found on the beach in smoothed chunks of man-made material, such as pottery or brick.

Wings

The double-shelled clam or mussel and the winged sycamore or ash seed take the number 2.

When you tune in to wings, you will zone in on the wings around you – naturally, birds and bats in flight and flying insects such as the dragonfly, butterfly and moth.

Fan

Depending on the shape, it may be more circular (number 1) or heart-shaped (number 3). Examples include the scallop shell, the cockle shell, the palm leaf, sweet pea flowers and some succulents.

Branch, Twig, Root or Stem

Count the number of buds, nodules or branching points, or opt for number 1, or the number that most resembles its shape. For example: you might have a branch that looks like a 7 or a length of vine that makes the squiggle of a 3.

Star-shape

Go by the number of points – so a five-petalled flower or a maple leaf, for example, takes the number 5. Look for this shape, too, in nut husks – some transform into a beautiful star when the husk curls back to release the nut.

For any shape that is 10 or more, such as ten faces on a piece of rock or ten petals on a flower, add together the number and reduce it. So, 10 would be 1 + 0 = 1, and 14 would be 1 + 4 = 5.

THE MEANING OF NUMBERS

The meanings set out here are ideas, starting points for your own interpretation. You may not need them; you may prefer to go with your instinctive response to the charm you hold. But what numerology does do is open up an alternative dimension of meaning. It's another way of appreciating your charm's detail and leading you toward a closer connection.

A choice of meanings for each number is given, representing different cultures and belief systems. For each number, a ruling planet and an element are included. For the astrologers among you, the ruling planets and their associated elements give a steer for further investigation of the number meanings. Do note that there is little agreement on all the planetary associations – although the Sun for 1, Moon for 2 and Venus for 6 appear consistently in virtually all sources.

NUMBER 1: ACTION AND UNITY

One is the beginning. The form of the number could be an upright person, a symbol of humanity. One therefore is the number of individuality, and in this sense it signifies action, focus, resources, movement and interaction with the world. Traditionally, number 1 is the circle, meaning oneness, or unity – which goes beyond the individual to the collective: the circle represents our connection with nature, to the divine and to collective consciousness. The circle is the shape of the ouroboros, the serpent swallowing its tale. Originating in ancient Egypt, the ouroboros signifies life cycles and renewal.

Pythagoras termed number 1 the monad, or divine intelligence, which the ancients expressed as a circle with a dot in the centre – the point of the creator's compass and the symbol of the Sun.

Planet: The Sun
Element: Fire

NUMBER 2: RELATIONSHIPS

Two is the number of duality, of doubles and pairs. It denotes partnerships, but also the tension of opposites. The number therefore expresses a relationship between two people or situations that are complementary or contrary. This number can mean negotiation and choices; a further interpretation is separation and return. As an almond shape, the 2 form suggests the mandorla (see vesica piscis, page 190), signifying a portal or that a decision or new partnership opens up new perspectives and experiences.

Planet: The Moon
Element: Water

NUMBER 3: THE CREATIVE FORCE

Three is the number of creation. The action of one and the negotiation of two gives three, the result or manifestation. Three relates to the triangle and is the first shape to be born from the vesica piscis (see page 190). Three denotes energy, power and fulfilment. In creative work, it often shows completing a first stage or phase – input is rewarded. The number is also linked with freedom, independence and perfection.

Planet: Jupiter

Element: Fire

NUMBER 4: ESTABLISHMENT

Four is the number of stability. It's associated with support, like the four legs of a table or a chair, suggesting security and firm foundations. There is a sense of logic and pragmatism with 4 – its evenness denotes order and balance. Other associations include loyalty, strength and teamwork. In ancient tradition, 4 represented truth and justice. Four also represents our reality – the structure of our experience, as in the four points of the compass, the four seasons and the four elements of earth, air, fire and water in Western thought.

Planet: Uranus

Element: Air

NUMBER 5: EXPERIENCE

Five is the number of human experience. Five is the human hand, the senses and, in some traditions, means growth, tests, readjustment, expansion and vitality. It's considered the number of the heart, which aligns with the Pythagorean meaning of 5 as the marriage number – the sum of 3 and 2, or the joining of male and female (3 was considered a male number and 2, female). The tarot card the Hierophant or High Priest is numbered 5, and historically it meant marriage – today it is often interpreted as unity. Five is the number of the pentagram, symbol of protection (see pages 195–196).

Planet: Mercury

Element: Air

NUMBER 6: HARMONY

Six is the number of perfection because it is the sum of its factors 1, 2 and 3: 1 + 2 + 3 = 6, and is associated with love, harmony and peace. Everything is balanced perfectly, bringing contentment and balance in life (the hexagon comprises two equal triangles). Other people are vitally important to sixes, given the number comprises three sets of two – the number of partnership. Additional meanings include sensitivity, imagination and idealism; as well as the need to see the best in a situation and to act for the good of all.

Planet: Venus
Element: Earth

NUMBER 7: INTUITION, MYSTERIES AND LUCK

As the highest single-digit prime number, seven was considered a special and mysterious number by the Pythagoreans. The meanings of 7 include dreams and precognition, intuition and spiritual seeking. Other interpretations include seeing the positive potential in a situation – a pragmatic twist on looking beyond the here and now. The combination of creative 3 and stable 4 also brings the meaning of wisdom and, according to Christian tradition, perfection – as in the making of the world in seven days. Seven is also considered a fortunate number; seventh sons (and occasionally, daughters) are still believed to be healers and clairvoyants, and seventh sons of seventh sons even more so.

Planet: Neptune
Element: Water

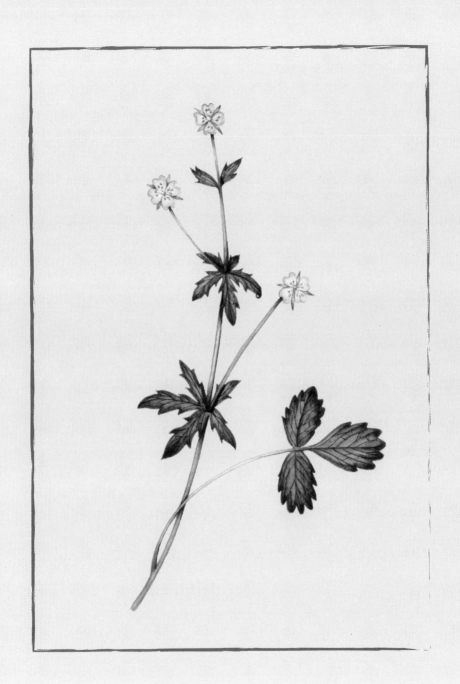

NUMBER 8: CHANGE

One number that many traditions agree about is 8, which means transformation and renewal. The octagon comprises two squares joining together – so the coming change brings together the stability of two lots of four in one empowering move. The shape also suggests the circle and the square: the square represents Earth and the circle, heaven. The octagon might eventually settle on one form or another, but as it exists now, it is in the process of shifting shape, and connects both worlds – the seen and the unseen. Additional meanings include enterprise, manifesting and dedication.

Planet: Saturn
Element: Earth

NUMBER 9: INTENSITY AND COMPLETION

Nine is the number of intensity. Nine comprises dynamic 3 trebled, and it brings with it all you have achieved and what you have accumulated so far; 9 reveals the fruits of your efforts, which may be sweet or bitter. Three 3s denote three cycles of creation; the third cycle is the last. The surge of energy and emotion that comes before completion leads you to seek answers, spiritual wisdom and a deeper sense of self-connection. This process of reflection leads to the beginning of a new cycle or life phase.

Planet: Mars
Element: Fire

Some systems see 10 as the final number after which the cycle begins again (1 + 0 = 1). In numerology the cycle ends at 9, the last of the single digits. Nine aligns with the concept of nine vibrations, or human characteristics, that each number represents.

THE NUMBER OF
CHARMS IN A GROUP

The number of charms you find together can also lead you into number interpretation. Naturally, you may find your charm with a multitude of others impossible to count – for example, one leaf in a carpet of fallen beech leaves or a sprig of lavender amid thousands of aromatic swaying stems. Other finds, however, may appear in small groups, such as pine cones, pieces of fallen bark and clusters of shells. When you get close, look for what lies around your chosen charm. You may see two, three, four or more other specimens in the same place. If so, look up the number on the previous pages for an interpretation. For a simpler meaning, a group can indicate family or friendships – so the invitation may be to develop ideas for the community, build a network or focus on the needs of your immediate family.

NUMBERS AS A
JOURNEY OF GROWTH

When you look at the charms you have collected, see what life stage they suggest. Does your twig look fresh or gnarled and brittle? If it's possible to break a small part of it, you'll see if you have dead wood or living wood. Are the leaves consistent in colour and shape or do they show signs of attack, such as discolouration, spotting or mildew? (Mildew appears as a white, powdery sprinkle on the leaf surface.) The condition of your charm can hold meaning for you. A young plant symbolizes a youthful situation, while a mature plant signifies strength and wisdom. An afflicted plant shows a time of tests and a need to persevere. We have a natural sympathy with the charms we choose, and they can often reveal something of our own situation.

We can see numbers 1 to 9 as a timeline for the growth cycle of plants. Add in zero (0), and we have the shape of the seed, which is pure potential at this stage. It needs nutrients and light to become number 1, the sprout, growing its first root. At number 2, it begins its journey toward the surface of the soil. Its root becomes established, and it grows its first pair of leaves. And so it progresses through the cycle, gaining more foliage and stalks, enduring the tests of the weather and potential infestation while it begins to bud. At 9, it flowers and/or bears fruit, and the cycle completes. If you can give your charm a growth number, you can add more meaning to the charm you hold.

SIGNIFICANT NUMBERS IN
CHARM-WORK: 3, 9, 7

Certain numbers reoccur in many historical healing charms and folk tales. The number 3 is a universal magical device for summoning power. Three relates to the element of fire, for dynamic energy (see page 212). Many charms and spells feature three magic ingredients, three days for it to work and reciting a charm three times.

Fairy tales are replete with threes: Goldilocks and the three bears, Cinderella and her two sisters, three wishes granted by a genie, and in the myriad threes of gifts, tasks or days for our heroines or heroes. The three is of course the story structure – the one as the beginning ("Once upon a time …"), two the middle or challenge, and three the completion – so they all lived happily ever after.

Three and its multiples appear consistently in charms in medieval texts. To the Anglo-Saxons, 9 was the magic number (the power of 3), which is the basis of the nine-herb charm, a folk remedy against infection and poison, found in *Lacnunga* ("Remedies"), a tenth-century manuscript.

The nine ingredients are: mugwort, plantain, lamb's cress (watercress), nettle, cockspur grass (or betony), chamomile, crab-apple, thyme (or chervil) and fennel. The nine ingredients had the power to disarm nine "poisons" or infections, from the "green poison" to the "poison-blister" – the infection and symptoms of snake bites. It was believed that evil spirits hid in the form of snakes, hence the need for magic. The herbs were pounded, and old soap and apple juice were mixed in to make an ointment for a wound. The healer sang a lengthy charm three times over each herb and the apple before preparing it, then sang it again into the patient's mouth, ears and into the wound before applying the ointment. Three and its multiples have great significance in this text: for example, there are nine herbs and nine poisons; the need to sing the charm three times over nine herbs; and the whole written charm runs to 63 lines.

Bald's *Leechbook*, a collection of remedies in Old English, includes a charm for a bad stomach, which involved eating pieces of holly boiled in milk (*Leechbook III*, LXIX). Then, the instructions say:

> *"... eat six slices, three in the morning and three in the evening, and after his food. Do so for nine days, longer if he is in need of it."*

The 9 was also used in counting charms, in which the spoken charm begins with the number 9 and decreases until there is nothing left – the perfect antidote for a boil or, as it was then known, a "furuncle".

This charm called "Against a Furuncle", from the *Lacnunga*, was to be chanted three times a day:

> *"Nine were Noththe's Sisters.*
> *Then the nine became eight*
> *and the eight became seven*
> *and the seven became six*
> *and the six became five*
> *and the five became four*
> *and the four became three*
> *and the three became two*
> *and the two became one*
> *and the one became none."*

The reason why 3 and 9 are the foundation of old charms and spells used today may be down to Germanic mythology, in which the world was tripartite: heaven, middle earth and the underworld. Their god Odin (Woden) hung from the Yggdrasil, the world ash tree, for nine nights in a state of spiritual suspension, after which he gained the gifts of prophecy and rune-reading.

The nine-herb charm says:

"... Woden took nine glory-twigs,
he smote then the adder that it flew apart into nine parts.
Now these nine herbs have power against nine evil spirits ..."

The "glory-twigs" are believed to refer to the runes, which Odin named after the herbs. Odin was also believed to be the father of charms – *galdrs fadir.*

In surviving written Anglo-Saxon charms, the number 7 appears less frequently than 3 and 9. However, charms collected from other sources do include 7 as the magic number of ingredients: Irish folklore names seven herbs of power:

"There are seven herbs that nothing natural or supernatural can injure; they are vervain, John's-wort, speedwell, eyebright, mallow, yarrow and self-help. But they must be pulled at noon on a bright day, near the full of the moon, to have full power."[27]

An old love charm from Sweden says if a young woman wanted to know her future lover she must venture out on Midsummer Eve and, in silence, pick seven different flowers from seven different meadows.

That night, if she placed the seven flowers under her pillow, she was sure to dream of her future soul mate.

In Kabbalah, a form of Jewish mysticism, a bracelet of seven knots is made to ward off the evil eye. Each knot is tied in a length of red thread while reciting the Ben Porat prayer of protection, then worn as a bracelet on the left wrist. The charm gives most protection when the person wearing it does not think negative thoughts, which can undermine its effectiveness.

Seven often arises as the number of days needed for a charm to work. As 7 represents the seven days of the week, it is not only a number of completion but symbolizes the process that creates the outcome: the initial intention, the necessary change that must occur, then the manifestation. The healing is complete, the wish granted. In Judaism, one example of the journey of the seven is "sitting *shiva*" (*shiva* means "seven"), a period of mourning for a departed loved one that lasts seven days.

In fairy tales, 7 appears as a period of seven days and seven years. In Beauty and the Beast, Beauty is given permission to visit her family for seven days after which time she must return. When she stays away longer, she finds the Beast almost dying of heartbreak because she had broken her vow. Snow White is seven years old when the magic mirror tells the evil queen that she is no longer the fairest in the land. Banished from the kingdom, Snow White is taken in by seven dwarfs, and our heroine can only fit on the seventh of the dwarfs' beds she tries for size. Psychologist Bruno Bettelheim suggests a current of pre-Christian belief underpins the tale – that Snow White, with her radiant beauty, represents the sun, and her seven dwarfs are the seven planets recognized by the ancients. This leads us again to the seven days of the week: Monday is the moon's day,

Tuesday is ruled by Mars, Wednesday by Mercury, Thursday by Jupiter, Friday by Venus, and Saturday by Saturn, while Sunday is self-explanatory.

These seven planets are named in this English protection charm, along with the planetary aspects of trine and sextile, and dragon's head and tail. This written charm was given to a man in 19th-century Burnley, Lancashire, who had suffered bad luck in the past. Fixed over the door of his house, it reads:

> *"Sun, Moon, Mars, Mercury, Jupiter, Venus, Saturn, Trine, Sextile, Dragon's Head, Dragon's Tail, I charge you to gard this house from all evils spirits whatever, and gard it from all Desorders, and from aney thing being taken wrangasly, and give this famaly good Ealth & Welth."*

And, finally, there was the tradition of the healing powers bestowed on the seventh son:

> *"When a seventh son is born, if an earth-worm is put into the infant's hand and kept there till it dies, the child will have power to charm away all diseases."*[28]

COUNTING CHARMS

Number charms, such as the furuncle charm mentioned on page 220, are found in many cultures and survive today in children's counting games and songs. There's "Eenie, meenie, miny, mo/Catch a tiger by the toe/If he screams, let him go/Eenie, meenie, miny, mo/Out goes you!" The children are counted, one for each word of the rhyme, but the child landed with "You" is out of the game. Then we have the song

"Ten Green Bottles" (sometimes sung as five or nine). It's interesting that green was once considered an unlucky colour, and in Anglo-Saxon times, elves – associated with green – took the blame for many a misfortune. Chickenpox was known as the water-elf disease, and there were herbal charms for salves for those who had been "elf-shot" (afflicted by shooting pains caused by arrows shot by invisible elves). As green represented supernatural power, the green bottles song may have its origins in an Anglo-Saxon banishing charm.

This Roman counting charm known as "The Spell of the Acorns", was once used to cure sore tonsils. The afflicted person had to gather nine acorns just before sunrise or sunset and recite this charm as they counted out each acorn, holding it between the thumb and middle finger:

"Nine little acorn sisters,

Eight little acorn sisters,

Seven little acorn sisters,

Six little acorn sisters,

Five little acorn sisters,

Four little acorn sisters,

Three little acorn sisters,

Two little acorn sisters,

One little acorn girl."

The chant and counting-out was repeated, but this time ending with:

"And there was no little acorn girl."[29]

The charm had to be recited accurately, without any mistakes, for it to work.

RITUAL
Counting Your Steps

When you walk, you can use your pace to count down to relaxation. Take a deep breath in and out, and begin to walk, getting into a light rhythm. Feel the vibration in your body and count your steps until your pace is steady and even. Then, intend that with each descending number, you will ease into relaxation and peace. Begin at 9, end at 0, take a breath (or pause walking if you need to) and repeat twice, so you do the countdown three times in total. Feel the calm.

Conclusion

I hope this book has inspired you to venture into nature and to receive all that nature offers with an open heart. Set out with a willingness to see and feel, and you will appreciate the sense of peace and connection that comes with being in the wild.

In the travellers' blessing that follows, two lines stirred me – the first, "May the sloughs fill up," because I needed to look up the meaning of "slough". It means swampy ground or a muddy hollow, so this is a plea for safety when crossing dangerous ground. The second line is, "May all good awake". When we step onto the sand, the shale, the path through the woods or simply the soft grass in our garden, we can feel nature's invitation to awaken to all life – an invitation that is always there for us, wherever and whoever we are.

May the hills lie low,
May the sloughs fill up,
In thy way.
May all evil sleep,
May all good awake,
In thy way.

"The Blessing of the Road", from *The Road to the Isles* by Kenneth Macleod.

Acknowledgements

With thanks to publisher Jo Lal, my agent Chelsey Fox, Michael W Young, and all those who have helped make this book a pleasure to write and, hopefully, read.

Image List

All illustrations by Lizzie Harper © 2021

Lizzie is a freelance botanical and natural history illustrator working traditionally in watercolour, pencil, and pen and ink.

Visit www.lizzieharper.co.uk to see more of her work.

* Cover illustrations

Endnotes

1   Ronald Hutton, *Pagan Britain*, p.309.

2   Museum of Witchcraft, Hare's Foot Charm: museumofwitchcraftandmagic.co.uk

3   Wendy L Rouse, *Charmed Lives: Charms, Amulets, and Childhood in Urban America, 1870–1940* (*The Journal of American Culture*, Volume 40, Number 1, March 2017).

4   Fairy stirrups and the piskie people of Cornwall: Charles Leyland, in *Gypsy Sorcery and Fortune Telling* (1891) quotes a Mr Hunt, who related this story in his *Popular Romances of the West of England* (1871, p.87).

5   Knotting of seven hairs in a horse's mane or cow tail: Thomas Johnson Westropp, *A Folklore Survey of County Clare*.

6   The left-handed whelk shell in the Science Museum, London: related in Annie Thwaite, *A History of Amulets in Ten Objects* (*Science Museum Group Journal*, Issue 11, Spring 2019; doi 10.15180; 191103).

7   Chris Gosden, *The History of Magic*, p.349.

8   Lisa Schneidau, *Botanical Folk Tales of Britain and Ireland*, p.96; a tale from Buckinghamshire rather than Grimm's fairy tale.

9   Ecologist Suzanne Simard, TED Talk: How Trees Talk to Each Other.

10 Stephen Harrod Buhner, *Plant Intelligence and the Imaginal Realm*, p.289.

11 Robert Graves, *The White Goddess*, p.189.

12 Jean Chevalier and Alain Gheerbrant, *The Penguin Dictionary of Symbols*, p.66.

13 Graves, p.385.

14 William Bottrell, *Traditions and Hearthside Stories of West Cornwall*, Volume 2. p.244.

15 James MacKillop, *A Dictionary of Celtic Mythology*, p.265.

16 Vance Randolph, *Ozark Magic and Folklore*, p.166.

17 E and M A Radford, *The Encyclopedia of Superstitions*, p.189.

18 Margaret Baker, *Discovering the Folklore of Plants*, p.41.

19 William Ralston, *Sorcery and Witchcraft: Songs of the Russian People*, p.359.

20 James Frazer, *The Golden Bough*, p.242.

21 Rev. Walter Gregor, *The Folk-Lore Journal*, Volume 4, Some Folk-Lore of the Sea, "The Storm", p.9.

22 Sir Walter Scott, *Minstrelsy of the Scottish Border*, Volume II, p.219.

23 *Folk-Lore*, Volume 25, p.372.

24 Laura Trethewey, *What Victorian-era seaweed pressings reveal about our changing seas*, 27 October 2020 in the Guardian [last accessed November 20, 2020].

25 Joseph Jacobs, *Celtic Fairy Tales*, XXV.

26 Lady Francesca Speranza Wilde, *Ancient Legends, Mystic Charms, and Superstitions of Ireland*, in Various Superstitions and Cures.

27 Francesca Speranza Wilde, "Ancient Legends, Mystic Charms, and Superstitions of Ireland", in *The Properties of Herbs and Their Use in Medicine*, p.185.

28 Wilde, in *Various Superstitions and Cures*, p. 203.

29 Acorn-counting charm from Marcellus Empiricus, a Latin medical writer, as related in Charles Leland's Etruscan Roman Remains in Popular Tradition, p.274.

Bibliography

Baker, Margaret, *Discovering the Folklore of Plants* (Shire Classics, 1996)

Bartlett, Sarah, *Knot Magic: A Handful of Powerful Spells Using Witches' Ladders and Other Magical Knots* (Quarto, 2020)

Bettelheim, Bruno, *The Uses of Enchantment: The Meaning and Importance of Fairy Tales* (Penguin, 1976)

Bonwick, James, *Irish Druids and Old Irish Religions* (Farran & Co, London 1894)

Bottrell, William, *Traditions and Hearthside Stories of West Cornwall*, Volume 2 (Beare and Son, 1873)

Buhner, Stephen Harrod, *Plant Intelligence and the Imaginal Realm* (Bear & Company, 2014)

Cadbury, Tabitha, *The Clarke Collection of Charms and Amulets in Scarborough Museum* (report, Scarborough Museum Library, 2010)

Chevalier, Jean and Gheerbrant, Alain; trans. John Buchanan-Brown, *The Penguin Dictionary of Symbols* (Penguin, 1996)

Coelho, Paul, *The Alchemist* (HarperCollins, 1995)

Culpeper, Nicholas, *Culpeper's Complete Herbal* (Foulsham edition, undated; first published 1653)

Dell, Christopher, *The Occult, Witchcraft and Magic: An Illustrated History* (Thames & Hudson, 2016)

Fontana, David, *The Secret Language of Symbols: A Visual Key to Symbols and Their Meanings* (Duncan Baird, 1993)

Frazer, James George, *The Golden Bough: A Study in Magic and Religion* (Macmillan, 1950)

Gosden, Chris, *The History of Magic: From Alchemy to Witchcraft, from the Ice Age to the Present Day* (Viking, 2020)

Graves, Robert, *The White Goddess: A Historical Grammar of Poetic Myth* (Faber, 1997)

Gregor, Rev. Walter, "Some Folk-Lore of the Sea", The *Folk-Lore Journal*, Volume 4, 1886

Harland, John, *Lancashire Folk-lore: Illustrative of the Superstitious Beliefs and Practices, Local Customs and Usages of the People of the County Palatine* (Library of Alexandria, 1876)

Hutton, Ronald, *Pagan Britain* (Yale University Press, 2014)

King, Graham, *The British Book of Spells & Charms: A Compilation of Traditional Folk Magic* (Troy Books, 2016)

Leland, Charles Godrey, *Etruscan Roman Remains in Popular Tradition* (New York, C. Scribner's sons, and London, T. F. Unwin, 1892)

Liabenow, Alonna, *The Significance of the Numbers Three, Four and Seven in Fairy Tales, Folklore, and Mythology* (Grand Valley State University, 2014)

Macleod, Kenneth, *The Road to the Isles* (Robert Grand & Son, 1927)

MacKillop, James, *A Dictionary of Celtic Mythology* (Oxford University Press, 2016)

MacTaggart, John, *The Scottish Gallovidian Encyclopedia* (Hamilton, Adams and Company, 1876)

Morris, Desmond, *Bodyguards: Protective Amulets and Charms* (Element, 1999)

Moorman, F W, *More Tales of the Ridings* (Elkin Mathews, 1920)

Radford, E and M A, *The Encyclopedia of Superstitions* (Helicon, 1995)

Ralston, William, *Sorcery and Witchcraft: Songs of the Russian People* (1872)

Randolph, Vance, *Ozark Magic and Folklore* (Dover, 1947)

Bibliography

Roud, Steve, *The Penguin Guide to the Superstitions of Britain and Ireland* (Penguin, 2003)

Schneidau, Lisa, *Botanical Folk Tales of Britain and Ireland* (The History Press, 2019)

Scott, Sir Walter, *Minstrelsy of the Scottish Border, Volume II* (Ballantyne, 1802)

Simard, Suzanne, TED Talk: How Trees Talk to Each Other

Storms, Godfrid, *Anglo-Saxon Magic* (Springer, first published 1948)

Thistelton-Dyer, T F, *The Mythic & Magickal Folklore of Plants* (Samhain Song Press, 2008. First published in 1889 as *The Folklore of Plants*)

Westropp, Thomas Johnson, "A Folklore Survey of County Clare" (published in *Folk Lore: Transactions of the Folklore Society*, 1910–1913)

Wilde, Lady Francesca Speranza, *Ancient Legends, Mystic Charms, and Superstitions of Ireland* (Ticknor and Co, 1887)